*1978*

THE PROTECTOR.

From a contemporary miniature painted on ivory, in the possession of the Author.

# THE TWO PROTECTORS:

## OLIVER AND RICHARD CROMWELL.

BY

### SIR RICHARD TANGYE.

**With Thirty-eight Illustrations.**

KENNIKAT PRESS
Port Washington, N. Y./London

**THE TWO PROTECTORS**

First published in 1899
Reissued in 1971 by Kennikat Press
Library of Congress Catalog Card No: 78-118504
ISBN 0-8046-1252-8

Manufactured by Taylor Publishing Company    Dallas, Texas

TO

FREDERIC  HARRISON,

WHOSE  ADMIRABLE  MONOGRAPH  ON

OLIVER  CROMWELL

HAS  DONE  SO  MUCH  TO  RECALL  THE

PRICELESS  SERVICES  RENDERED

TO  HIS  COUNTRY  BY

ENGLAND'S  "CHIEF  OF  MEN."

# TO THE LORD GENERAL CROMWELL,

## 1652.

CROMWELL, our chief of men, who through a cloud
　　Not of war only, but detractions rude,
　　Guided by faith and matchless fortitude,
　　To peace and truth thy glorious way hast plough'd,
And on the neck of crownèd Fortune proud
　　Hast rear'd GOD'S trophies, and His work pursued,
　　While Darwen stream with blood of Scots embrued,
　　And Dunbar field resounds thy praises loud,
And Worcester's laureat wreath.　Yet much remains
　　To conquer still ; Peace hath her victories
　　No less renown'd than War ; new foes arise
Threat'ning to bind our souls with secular chains.
　　Help us to save free conscience from the paw
　　Of hireling wolves, whose gospel is their maw.

*Milton.*

# PREFACE.

CROMWELL'S first speech in Parliament was delivered in 1629. It was a protest against the Romanising of the Church of England by Laud and other Church dignitaries.

The House resolved itself into a "Grand Committee of Religion," and was proceeding to inquire into the doings of these men, when Charles suddenly dissolved it ; and during the next eleven years Popery, under Laud, had a free hand. The ears of Nonconformists were cut off and their cheeks branded with red-hot irons, their property confiscated, and their bodies thrown into prison. The Inquisition, under the guise of the Star Chamber, was in full force, and Religious and Civil Liberty were non-existent.

It was from this terrible condition that OLIVER CROMWELL and his colleagues rescued England, and thereby earned the undying gratitude of all succeeding generations.

R. T.

April 25th, 1899.

# NOTE.

*It will be convenient to remember that in the Commonwealth times— and indeed, down to 1752 — New Year's Day in England was the 25th March. In Scotland the year began with January since 1600.*

# CONTENTS.

# LIST OF ILLUSTRATIONS.

## AUTHORITIES CONSULTED.

Rushworth, Thurloe, Whitelocke, *Cromwelliana*, Ludlow, Sprigge's *Anglia Rediviva*, 1647, " Carrion" Heath, Mark Noble, Carlyle, Green's *Short History*, MS. Journal of the Protectoral House of Lords and other original MSS., and Frederic Harrison's *Oliver Cromwell* (Macmillan, 1895), etc., etc.

**THE HOROSCOPE.**

From a rare print in the Author's Collection.

# CHAPTER I.

ON "April 24th, 1599, 15 h: 46 m: P.M.," * there was born into the world at Huntingdon a veritable man-child, Oliver, the son of Robert and Elizabeth Cromwell. The future Protector came from good families on both sides, Robert Cromwell being the son of Sir Henry Cromwell, known as the Golden Knight of Hinchinbrook ; and his wife, Elizabeth (so named after the great Queen whose eventful life was now drawing to a close), being the sister of Sir Thomas Steward, who had succeeded to the estates which came to the family at the Dissolution of the Monasteries. The great-uncle of Oliver's mother, Robert Steward, D.D., was a prototype of the famous Vicar of Bray; he was the last Catholic Prior of Ely, an office which he had held for twenty years, and at the Dissolution became the Protestant Dean, a position which he held for a similar period. The founder of the Protector's family was Sir Richard Cromwell, nephew of Thomas Cromwell, Earl of Essex, who so zealously carried out the orders of his royal master, Henry VIII., in suppressing and despoiling the Monasteries, and lost his head for his pains.

* Inscription on a picture of Oliver Cromwell in which his horoscope is given.

This Thomas Cromwell was styled the *Malleus Monachorum,* or "Hammer of Monasteries," and much of the havoc wrought by him amongst the abbey churches of the kingdom has been wrongly attributed to Oliver. Sir Henry Cromwell, the Golden Knight, and after him his brother, Sir Oliver, lived in a stately palace at Hinchinbrook, which the former had built, and where he had entertained the Queen in 1564.

Sir Oliver, not to be outdone by his brother in magnificent hospitality to Royalty, entertained King James I. for two days, on his accession to the throne, and ruined himself by foolish extravagance. He became godfather to young Oliver, and lived to see him Lord Protector of the Commonwealth. But the influences that determined Oliver's adherence to the Puritan party had no weight with his relatives, nearly all of whom remained Royalists, many taking active service in the King's army.

James I. did not favour Puritanism or Puritans ; he had been accustomed to be treated by his Court-sycophants as though he were a demi-god, and the Puritans, down-trodden and straitened in every movement as they were, refused to render to the creature what belonged only to the Creator. At the beginning of the 17th century it had become clear to all men that a crisis in religious matters was fast approaching. Large numbers of the hard-working clergy became greatly alarmed at the encouragement given to extreme ritual by the greater number of the bishops and other dignitaries of the Church. They determined to make a supreme effort to obtain relief, and petitions to the King were prepared in all parts of the country, one, the *Millennary Petition,* being signed by nearly a thousand clergymen.  The petitioners pointed out that practices savouring strongly of the Romish ceremonial were fast creeping in, and that clergymen who failed to fall in with them were frowned upon by their superiors in the Church, and they prayed the King that, as head of the Church, he would grant them relief.  Accordingly, in January, 1603-4, the Hampton Court Conference was called, at which the King presided, being very much in his element.  The " dissentient " clergy were represented by four learned doctors from the two Universities, and the Church by all its most distinguished dignitaries. Witnesses were called on either side, and the King made many learned speeches, in the end dismissing the appellants with contumely, telling them that if they failed to conform he would " harry them out of the country."  And so the good seed of English liberty was sown by Royal hands.

**Robert Cromwell.** As a consequence of the extrava-gance of his father and uncle, the fortune which came to Robert Cromwell, a younger son, was a very moderate one, consisting of a small estate at Huntingdon, and of the great tithes of Hartford.  The income from these sources, supple-mented by his wife's jointure, amounted to a sum equal to £1,200 a year of the present day.

His portrait represents him as a somewhat proud and austere man, but he appears to have been a good father and an exemplary citizen, taking his full share of public work.

The Cavaliers and aristocrats of later date thought to disparage the Lord Protector and his father by describing them as " brewers," but although Parliament has refused to place a statue of Oliver in its rightful place amongst the Kings of England, we hear no more of his having been a brewer, because some of the ornaments of the House of Lords swam into that Chamber on beer, and still maintain their lordly state by its sale.

But, like many other great men, it is to his mother that Oliver undoubtedly owes his many great qualities. Her devout and prayerful spirit, and her great strength of character were largely reproduced in her distinguished son.

**Elizabeth Cromwell.**  Robert Cromwell married Elizabeth, daughter of William Steward of Ely, and widow of William Lynne ; the former, with his only child, died within a year of their marriage. Noble says of them, " They were persons of great worth, remarkable for living upon a small fortune with decency, and maintaining a large family by their frugal circumspection." * Mrs. Cromwell survived her husband thirty-seven years ; she was a careful, prudent mother, and brought up her daughters in such a way as to secure for them honourable and worthy settlement in life. She was a great favourite with her husband's relations, and especially with her son's godfather, Sir Oliver Cromwell. On looking at her portrait, one is not long left in doubt as to the origin of the Protector's strong features ; evidently she had a strong will, and knew how to carry it into effect. Between her illustrious son and herself there existed a bond of union of unusual depth and strength ; on all occasions Oliver displayed an

* Noble's *House of Cromwell.*

OLIVER CROMWELL, AT THE AGE OF FIVE YEARS.
From the original painting at Hinchinbrook.

unbounded affection for her, and when he assumed supreme power, insisted upon her living with him at Whitehall. But amidst all the grandeur of her surroundings she never lost her native simplicity of character. Her anxiety on behalf of her son was constant and intense, and Ludlow says, "At the sound of a musket she would often be afraid her son was shot, and could not be satisfied unless she saw him once a day at least." She died on the 16th November, 1654, and Thurloe, writing on the following day, records, "My Lord Protector's mother, of ninety-four years old, died last night. A little before her death she gave my Lord her blessing in these words, 'The Lord cause His face to shine upon you, and comfort you in all your adversities, and enable you to do great things for the glory of your Most High God, and to be a relief unto His people. My dear son, I leave my heart with thee. A good night!'"

Such were the parents, and such the up-bringing of one who became "the greatest, because the most typical Englishman of all time."

Oliver referred to his own origin in his speech to his first Parliament, September 12, 1654, when he said, "I was by birth a gentleman, neither living in any considerable height nor yet in obscurity"; and Milton says of him, "He was descended of a house noble and illustrious."

# CHAPTER II.

THE first portrait of Oliver, which shows him as a boy of five, bright and open-faced, is at Hinchinbrook, and with the exception of a curious little engraving, to which I will presently refer, there is not another representation of him until after the Civil War had commenced.

The engraving referred to is a very quaint one. It represents an ancient dominie in his gown, birch rod in hand, ready to impress his admonitions on the youthful minds (or backs) of the two boys, also in gowns, who cling to his robe. On a high shelf are a number of school books, quite out of reach of the boys. The dominie is Dr. Beard of Huntingdon, and the two boys are Oliver Cromwell and his cousin, John Hampden. The birch rod evidently left no unpleasant memories on Oliver's mind, for, until the Doctor's death in 1632, they were very intimately associated as fellow Justices of the Peace, and in other public capacities, in Huntingdon ; and it is recorded that in Oliver's first speech in Parliament he referred to his old friend and schoolmaster.

**Oliver at Cambridge, 1616.** From the Grammar School of his native town, Oliver removed to Cambridge, where, on the 23rd of April, 1616, two days before his seventeenth birthday, he was entered a Fellow Commoner of Sidney Sussex College ; and

DR. BEARD.

SCHOOLMASTER TO OLIVER CROMWELL AND JOHN HAMPDEN.

it is a noteworthy fact that while young Cromwell was thus commencing his college career another of England's greatest men had just entered the dark valley, for on that very day, in the quiet old town of Stratford-on-Avon, Shakespeare passed to his rest.

And now the training in Puritan principles which Oliver had received from his old master, Dr. Beard, was to be continued at Cambridge, for Sidney Sussex College had been denounced by Laud as a hotbed of Puritanism, and its head, Dr. Samuel Ward (one of the translators of the Bible) was a pronounced Protestant.

It is not known precisely when Oliver left Cambridge, but as his father died in June of 1617, and he was the only son, it is more than probable that his college career was terminated by that event.

But although Oliver's stay at Cambridge was of such short duration, he always retained a strong regard for the University, and expressed it by an order (1st July, 1652) directed to all officers and soldiers under his command, forbidding them "to quarter any officer or soldier in any of the colleges, halls, or other houses belonging to that University, or to offer any injury or violence to any of the students or members of it ; and this at their peril." *

**Mythical stories of Oliver's boyhood.** It usually happens that when a great man dies, and is consequently unable to refute tales respecting himself, a plentiful crop, more or less mythical in character, quickly springs up, and Oliver was no exception to the rule. " Carrion Heath," as Carlyle dubs him, declares in his rancorous

* Noble.

pamphlet *Flagellum,* that Oliver spent much of his boyhood in robbing dove-cots and orchards, and that he was known to his neighbours as *Apple-dragon ;* while another account says that Dr. Beard soundly flogged him for having declared that in a dream a gigantic figure drew aside his bed curtains and told him that he would become the greatest person in the kingdom, but that his prophetic tongue omitted the word *King.* On another occasion the boy Oliver is said to have taken part in a play in which it fell to him to assume a paper crown, and to say :

> " Methinks I hear my noble parasites
> Styling me Cæsar, or great Alexander."

It is also related that when Prince Charles rested at Hinchinbrook on his way to London, in 1604—he being about four years old, Oliver—who was a year older, met him for the first time, and in a quarrel caused the blood to flow from the royal nose. Noble, in his *House of Cromwell,* in giving this story, adds : "This was looked upon as a bad presage for that king when the Civil Wars commenced." *

But even if these stories were true, and most of them are extremely doubtful, they would be perfectly inoperative in forming the character of such a man as Oliver Cromwell.

As to Oliver's intellectual attainments, it is stated

---

* The Rev. Mark Noble was the author of one of the best-known histories of Cromwell and his family, first published in two volumes about the middle of last century. The Rev. Mark, who is styled " *My rev. imbecile friend* " by Carlyle, makes the mistake of thinking himself more important than the subject of his biography, for he puts *his own* portrait as the frontispiece of the *first* volume, and that of Oliver in the second.

that he excelled chiefly in mathematics ; that he attained to a good knowledge of Latin, conversationally, is clear from the circumstance that he carried on a negotiation with a foreign Ambassador in that tongue. Bishop Burnet, who was nothing if not spiteful, declared that Cromwell spoke Latin "viciously and scantily." Edmund Waller, who was well able to judge, says that Oliver "was very well read in Greek and Roman story." We know that in after life he was the generous friend and patron of learning and learned men, and that Milton entertained a profound respect for him.

But it is impossible to rise from a perusal of his letters and speeches without being impressed with the sense that, whatever books he may or may not have read, he had thoroughly mastered what, in modern *parlance*, has been called "the human document." And although many men have made large collections of books without having mastered their contents, it is not likely that Oliver, with his intensely practical mind, would have been content with knowing the titles only of "the noble collection of books" which he had made.

Little is known of Oliver as a young man, but " when we first reach authentic utterances of Cromwell himself, we meet with a spirit of intense religious earnestness. The whole of his surroundings in childhood and youth tended to that direction. A Puritan mother, a serious father, a zealous Puritan schoolmaster, a Puritan college, under a Puritan head, his father's premature death and his own early responsibilities, his veneration for his mother,"*

* F. Harrison's *Cromwell*, p. 15 (Macmillan, 1895).

all operated in preparing him for the intensely serious
part he was so soon to be called upon to play in the
great national drama.

**A Confirmed**      Of this period of Oliver's life, Carlyle
**Puritan.**      writes,* he "naturally consorted henceforth with the Puritan clergy . . . zealously
attended their ministry . . . consorted with
Puritans in general, many of whom were gentry of
his own rank, some of them nobility of much higher
rank.  A modest, devout man, solemnly intent 'to
make his calling and his election sure,' to whom, in
credible dialect, the Voice of the Highest had spoken ;
whose earnestness, sagacity, and manful worth
gradually made him conspicuous in his circle among
such.  The Puritans were already numerous.  John
Hampden, Oliver's cousin, was a devout Puritan,
John Pym the like, Lord Brook, Lord Say, Lord
Montague ; Puritans in the better ranks, and in
every rank, abounded.  Already, either in conscious
act or in clear tendency, the far greater part of the
serious thought and manhood of England had
declared itself Puritan."

**Marries**      On August 22nd Oliver married the
**Elizabeth**      daughter of Sir James Bourchier, a
**Bourchier,**
**1620.**      City magnate, and for thirty-eight
years (until his death), she was his faithful and devoted
wife.  Fifty-four years after their marriage, John
Milton was laid to rest in the same church of St.
Giles', Cripplegate.

Almost all the portraits of the Protectress represent her with a monkey, and although Mark Noble
gives a preposterous explanation of its presence, it is

* *Letters and Speeches*, vol. i. p. 53.

Elizabeth Daughter of S.r James Bowsher
Wife of Oliver Cromwell commonly call'd
JOAN or Postscress Cromwell.

ELIZABETH.

WIFE OF OLIVER CROMWELL.

not known what its real significance is. It is related
that when an infant at Hinchinbrook on a visit, an
ape one day took Oliver out of his cradle and, to the
terror of his mother and the attendants, carried him
on to the leads of the house. Beds were brought
out and laid on the ground lest the animal should
drop the child, but it brought him down safely.
As it was not an unusual thing for a monkey
to be kept in great houses, it is possible the Protectress had a kindness for an animal which had dealt
so gently with one who was destined to become her
husband.

**Accession of
Charles First,
March, 1625.** It was with a feeling of great relief
that the nation received the news of
the death of the royal pedant, James
I., and all eyes were turned with hope to his successor, Charles I. But it was not long before serious
doubts began to be entertained as to the course
political events were likely to take. In May, the ill-
starred marriage of Charles to Henrietta Maria, sister
of the French King, took place, and it soon became
evident that Charles was but a puppet in the hands
of Villiers, the reckless and profligate Duke of
Buckingham.

Parliament met in June, but—led by men like
Hampden, Selden, Eliot, Pym, and Coke, men who
knew their power and were determined to exert it—
having committed the unpardonable sin of thwarting
the designs of Buckingham by refusing the supplies
for carrying his projects into effect, it was in less
than two months dissolved.

Buckingham's foreign policy was, however, carried
out without the sanction of Parliament, involving

Charles in overwhelming debt and compelling him
to summon his second Parliament in the following
year; but after a stormy session of less than three
months it also was dissolved, the Commons being
inflexible in their determination to vote no money
the expenditure of which was to be independent of
them.

During the next two or three years Charles
plunged deeper into the mire; his foreign expedi-
tions all ended in failure, and he had succeeded in
exasperating the nation by his illegal exactions.
Money was raised by forced loans, which he
endeavoured to make acceptable by styling them
"benevolences" *—by arbitrary arrests and fines for

* "*Benevolences.*"—Here is a copy of one of these documents, addressed to " Our Trustie and welbeloved Robert
Maxwell of Throwley, Esquire, Privy Seale 25 November 1625
to borrow £20." (Numbered 39.)

" By the King.

"Trustie and welbeloved, We greet you well. Having
observed in the Presidents and customes of former times,
That the Kings and Queenes of this our Realme upon extraordinary occasions have used either to resort to those con-
tributions which arise from the generality of subjects, or to
the private helpes of some well-affected in particular by way
of loane; In the former of which Courses as we have no
doubt of the love and affection of Our people when they shall
again assemble in Parliament, so for the present we are
enforced to proceed in the latter course for supply of some
portions of Treasure for divers publique services, which without manifold inconveniences to Us and Our Kingdomes, cannot be deferred: And therefore this being the first time that
We have required anything in this kind, We doubt not but
that We shall receive such a testimony of good affection from
you (amongst other of Our subjects) and that with such
alacrity and readiness, as may make the same so much the
more acceptable, especially seeing that We require but that
of some, which few men would deny a friend, and have a mind
resolved to expose all Our earthly fortune for preservation of

imaginary offences, and in other unlawful ways. But it was all in vain; confusion and general disorganisation reigned in every department of State, and, *nolens volens*, Parliament had to be summoned again.

**Enter Oliver, M.P., 1628.** Charles's third Parliament met on the 17th March, 1628, and Oliver Cromwell sat in it as Member for Huntingdon. But it was evident from the outset that this Assembly would be even less amenable to the King's wishes than its predecessor, mainly composed as it was of well-known opponents of the Court, many of whom had suffered imprisonment and heavy pecuniary exactions at the hands of the King.

It was during this Parliament that Wentworth—afterwards Earl of Strafford—fell away from the popular party.

Parliament was dissolved on the 2nd of March, 1629, but not before it had laid the foundations of an entirely new form of government—personal rule giving place to that of Parliament. The Petition of Right had been adopted, and henceforth no

the Generall; The summe which we require of you by vertue of these presents is Twentie pounds which We do promise in the name of Us, Our Heires and Successours to repay to you or your Assignes within eighteene moneths after the payment thereof unto the Collector. The person that We have appointed to collect is Sr. Symon Weston K^nt. or Thomas Crumpton Esq : to whose hands We doe require you to send it within twelve dayes after you have received this Privy Seale, which together with the Collectors acquittance, shalbe sufficient warrant unto the Officers of Our Receipt for the repayment thereof at the time limited. Given under Our Privy Seale at Hampton Court the Twentith daye of November in the first yeare of Our raigne of England, Scotland, France and Ireland, 1625."—*From an original in the Author's Collection.*

supplies would be granted until grievances had been fully discussed.

**Oliver's First Parliamentary Speech, 11th Feb., 1628=29.** It was during the Session of 1629 that Oliver Cromwell delivered his first speech, and in view of present-day discussions upon Romish practices in the Church of England, his remarks have a special significance. It was in the Committee on Religion that the speech was delivered, and happily an interesting fragment of it has been preserved. He said: "He had heard by relation from one Dr. Beard (his old schoolmaster) that Dr. Alablaster had preached flat Popery at Paul's Cross, and that the Bishop of Winchester had commanded him, as his Diocesan, he should preach nothing to the contrary. Mainwaring, so justly censured in this House for his sermons, was by the same Bishop's means preferred to a rich living. If these are the steps to Church-preferment, what are we to expect?"

Oliver returned to Huntingdon, and was to have no more Parliamentary experiences for eleven years. His first act of rebellion against Charles was committed in 1631, when he was fined £10 for refusing to go up to be knighted at Westminster at the King's Coronation.

**Star Chamber, 1629=1640.** From 1629 to 1640 there had been no Parliament, and the country had been ruled by the Star Chamber under Strafford and Laud. Ship money and other illegal taxes had been levied, and men had their ears cropped because they dared to disagree with the Archbishop on matters of religion. Had Laud been a prophet, and could he have foreseen that his own ears (with his

THE UPPER AND LOWER HOUSES OF PARLIAMENT.

TIME OF CHARLES I.

head) would also be cropped at no distant date, perhaps he might have doubted that religion could be advanced by the use of the executioner's shears.

**Prynne, Burton, & Bastwick.** There is in existence a rare pamphlet, of 31 pp., dated 1637, giving a full account of the trial of Prynne, Burton and Bastwick. Prynne was tried—or rather condemned, for there was no trial—in the Star Chamber, on the 14th June, for an alleged libel on Bishop Laud. Having received a subpœna requiring him to appear in the Star Chamber to answer the charge against him, he obeyed, taking with him a copy of the information ; whereupon he was ordered to prepare his answer, but being immediately committed to prison, and denied the use of pen, ink, and paper, he was unable to do so. Counsel was assigned to him, but would not come, and he, being in prison, could not go to him. Then upon motion made, the Court authorised Prynne to go to the Counsel, but before he could do so, he was again consigned to prison. A second motion for pens and ink was successful, and he drew up his answer, acting under advice of Counsel, and, Prynne says, "payd him twice for drawing it." The Court refused to accept his "answer," on the plea of its not having been signed by Counsel, and on Prynne calling the latter he excused himself, saying that he "feared giving your Honours distaste," whereupon Prynne, in open Court, branded him as a coward. The Lord Keeper refused the "answer," remarking it was "too long," and demanded that he should plead "guilty or not guilty."

In vain did Prynne show that he had done his utmost to answer the charge against him, and that he could not compel his Counsel to put it in due form by appending his signature. "Well, hold your peace," said this scoundrel judge, "your answer comes too late." Then the same tragical farce was gone through with the other two defendants, after which the Lord Keeper (Cottington) passed this diabolical sentence : "I condemn these three men to lose their ears in the Pallace-yard, at Westminster : to be fined £5,000 a man to his Majestie : and to perpetual imprisonment in three remote places of the Kingdom, namely, the Castles of Carnarvon, Cornwall, and Lancaster."

The Lord Chief "Justice" (Finch)* added to this sentence : "Mr. Prynne to be *stigmatised* in the cheekes with two letters (S. & L.) for a Seditious Libeller, to which all the Lords agreed." The sentence was carried out in the most brutal manner, the executioner cutting Prynne's ears so close as to tear away a part of the cheek with them. For details of the sickening business, see Carlyle, vol. i., p. 136.

Prynne's ears had once before been cut off, but by favour of the executioner he was permitted to have them sewn on again. This was referred to by the vile Lord Chief "Justice" (Finch) when the prisoner was brought up for trial on the new charge.

This is how the proceedings opened : "Between 8 and 9 o'clock in the morning (14th June) the Lords being sett in their places in the Court of Starre-Chamber, and casting their eyes upon the Prisoners, then att the Barr, Sr. Jno. Finch (Ch. Justice of the

* This inhuman monster had to fly the country for his life at a later date, because of his share in this day's proceedings.

Common Pleas) began to speak after this manner : " I had thought Mr. Prynne had had no eares, but methinks he hath eares " ; which caused many of the Lords to take the stricter view of him ; and for their better satisfaction, the Usher of the Court was commanded to turne up his haire, and shew his eares : upon the sight whereof the Lords were displeased they had been formerly no more cut off ; and cast out some disgraceful words of him. To which Mr. Prynne replied : "My Lords, there is never a one of your Honours, but would be sorry to have your eares as mine are."

The Lord Keeper replied, "In good faith he is somewhat sawcy."

Mr. Prynne : "I hope yr Honours will not be offended, I pray God give you eares to heare."

Mr. Prynne observing that some Prelates were sitting on the Bench, moved that they should be dismissed, stating that it was "contrary to equity that they who are our Adversaries should be our Judges : Therefore we humbly crave that they may be *expunged out of the Court.*" (A splendid phrase !) But of course it was refused, the Lord Keeper observing that it was "a sweet motion." But the days of Prelatical tyranny were nearing their end.

As already stated, the prisoners were not allowed to put in their defence, but with the "justice" characteristic of these infamous clerical and judicial persecutors, Laud, one of the complainants, was not only permitted to sit on the Bench with the Judges, but also to deliver a scurrilous harangue against the defendants. This speech was afterwards published in a small quarto vol. of 77 pp., and dedicated to the

Master tyrant, Charles I.*  The dedication begins
with :  "I had no purpose to come in print, but
your Majesty commands it, and I obey."   And then,
with the cowardice common to all bullies, he says :
"I humbly desire Your Sacred Majesty to protect
me from the undeserved calumny of these men,
whose mouths are spears and arrows, and their
tongues a sharp sword ; though their foolish mouths
have already called for their own stripes" (and *loss of
ears,* he might have added).   The unctuous dedication ends with a prayer that God would "bless
your Majestie, your Royal Consort, and your Hopefull Posterity."   Charles II. and James II., " Hopefull
Posterity" !

---

* This vol. (which is in the Author's collection) is unique,
being a presentation copy with Laud's inscription on the fly-leaf,
"For Dr. Sterne," and " Ex dono Reverendissimi authoris"
in Dr. Sterne's handwriting.   Dr. Sterne was Laud's Chaplain, and afterwards Archbishop of York.   At p. 45 Laud has
written a note with reference to Queen Elizabeth ; "at her
coming to Cambridge order was taken beforehand by the
Chancellor that all the Communion Tables should be sett that
way.   See Mr. Stokes (who was then Bedell and Register of
the University), his relation of that entertainment."   The
important point being whether the table should stand north
and south with its side against the people, or with its *end*
towards them.

# CHAPTER III.

IN 1636, Sir Thomas Steward died, leaving Oliver considerable property in Ely, to which city he then removed, living in a house, still standing, next to St. Mary's Church. Here he continued to reside with his family until the final removal to London in 1647.

A well-known picture represents Oliver and a number of friends about to embark in a vessel for America, but prevented by the presentation of an Order in Council forbidding them to leave the country. There is no foundation for this story, which in itself is altogether improbable, as Cromwell and the other leaders of the Puritan party had already laid their plans for carrying on the struggle against the arbitrary acts of the King, which were daily becoming more intolerable.

**The Grand Remonstrance, 22nd Nov., 1641.** It is probable that this tradition arose from Cromwell's remark to Lord Falkland after the passing of the Grand Remonstrance. Said he, "If the Remonstrance had been rejected, I would have sold all I had the next morning, and never have seen England any more ; and I know there are many other honest men of this same resolution."

**The Short Parliament.** Strafford's policy of "Thorough" in Ireland, and Laud's policy of ear-cropping and cheek-branding in England, had failed to satisfy the country, or to bring peace and supplies of money to Charles. The culmination of the King's troubles was reached when the Scotch "covenant" rebellion broke out in 1638 ; vainly he struggled on, and even Strafford was compelled at length to advise the summoning of Parliament. It met on 13th April, 1640, but because it attacked the policy of the King instead of voting supplies—Charles wanting money, not advice—it only lived twenty-three days. Oliver sat in this Parliament as Member for Cambridge.

**The Long Parliament, Oliver æt 41.** But another war breaking out in Scotland, Charles had perforce to call his "Faithful Commons" together again (the Lords did not count), and on the 3rd of November of the same year the Long Parliament assembled at Westminster, and continued to sit till Oliver himself dissolved it in 1653. Great efforts were made to keep Cromwell out of the representation of Cambridge, but they were unsuccessful, and he had the satisfaction of receiving as a colleague a brother Puritan in place of a Courtier.

**John Lilburne.** And here John Lilburne first appears on the scene. John had been secretary to Prynne of Star Chamber fame, and had been punished by "whipping with two hundred stripes from Westminster to the Fleet Prison," where he remained. His offence was publishing of libels (so-called by the Court party), and Oliver took up his cause. Years after, John quarrelled with his defender, the Protector, but that was nothing unusual with him, for was it not said of him that " *if no one was left in the world but John Lilburne, John would quarrel with Lilburne, and Lilburne with John !* "

Cromwell was also appointed on the Committee to consider the cases of Prynne, Burton and Bastwick, and other " crop-eared" victims of Laud's tyranny. These clerical and other tyrants had a very simple way of finding nicknames for their victims ; first they cut off their ears and then they called them " crop-eared." But the operation produced a bitter crop of well-deserved troubles for the tyrants before many years had passed.

**Oliver clotbed by " an ill coun= try tailor."** It was on the occasion of Oliver's defence of Lilburne that Sir Philip Warwick, M.P. for Radnor, gave the following description of Oliver's personal appearance. " The first time I ever took notice of Mr. Cromwell was in the very beginning of the Parliament held in November, 1640 ; when I vainly thought myself a courtly young gentleman, for we Courtiers valued ourselves much upon our good clothes ! I came into the House one morning well clad ; and perceived a gentleman speaking, whom I knew not, very ordinarily apparelled ; for it was a plain cloth suit, which seemed to have been made by an ill country tailor ; his linen was plain and not very clean, and I remember a speck or two of blood upon his little band, which was not much larger than his collar. His hat was without a hatband. His stature was of a good size ; his sword stuck close to his side ; his countenance swoln and reddish, his voice sharp and untuneable, and his eloquence full of fervour. For the subject matter would not bear much of *reason,* it being on behalf of a servant of Mr. Prynne's (Jno. Lilburne), who had dispersed Libels. I sincerely profess, it lessened much my reverence unto that Great Council, for this gentleman was very much hearkened unto."

Cromwell was no longer merely the interested ob-
server of the proceedings of Parliament ; he speedily
began to take an active part in all questions where
the rights of conscience and of oppressed individuals
were concerned. The victims of the Star Chamber
found in him a powerful friend, and, a grasping
landowner at Huntingdon having enclosed some
common land, Oliver espoused their cause with such
warmth before the Committee appointed to deal with
such matters, that he was repeatedly called to order
by the Chairman, Hyde, afterwards Earl Clarendon.

Great questions very soon claimed the deepest
attention of Parliament, Cromwell taking his full
share in their discussion. The Bill for the abolition
of Episcopacy, "root and branch," was the occasion
of stormy debate, in the course of which Oliver was
interrupted with calls of "to the bar." "But here, in
Episcopacy, was sounded the critical note which
ultimately rallied to the King so large a portion of the
people and the gentry. From that hour the King
represented the Church." *

Cromwell also seconded the motion for the
Annual Parliaments Bill, which ultimately resolved
itself into an Act establishing Triennial Parliaments.
In conjunction with Sir Harry Vane he also prepared
a Bill for the abolition of Episcopacy, upon which
occasion Hyde finally joined the Court party. The
extirpation of Laudism and the defence of Puritanism
were the causes which chiefly enlisted Oliver's most
earnest co-operation.

Here is a curious little scrap written as early as
1641, from the quiet of Cambridge, where events in

* F. Harrison.

the world outside were beginning to make a stir ; it is strange that it should have been so long preserved.*
The letter contains Greek and Latin quotations, which have been translated in this copy : " *What news, sweet Mr. Knyvett ?* † *What is our destiny ? In one word, there is uneasiness, are we lost ? or has that bird of Juno sung to us ' all will be well,' for I hear we are now in the most critical times ? If you love us, be not now silent. We here only desire two things, a settled Commonwealth and your letters.*

" *Mr. Peckover is your servant, and so is*
" *Your assured friend,*
" *Franc. Colfer.*
" *Cambridge, May 4th, 1641.*"

Events were marching on.  On 6th Nov., 1641, the Earl of Essex was ordered to raise the trainbands for the defence of the Kingdom, and it was further ordered " that this power should continue until the Parliament should take further order." A clear notice to the King that the Parliament had now an army.

On the 22nd, the debate on the Grand Remonstrance was ended, the motion being carried by a majority of eleven only, amid a scene of wild confusion, during which members drew their swords, and seemed about to begin the war on the floor of the House.

**Arrest of the Five Members, Jan. 4th, 1641=2.**  And now the King made a fatal mistake which raised the whole country against him.  He determined to seize the persons of those Members of Parliament whom he

---

\* In the Author's collection.

† Probably the Th : Knyvett referred to in Carlyle, vol. i., pp. 171, 175.

considered the most dangerous to his cause. On the
3rd January he sent a message to the House demanding
that five members named by him should be delivered
up to him as traitors. The House temporised and sent
an evasive reply. "But, ill satisfied with this, Charles
the next day proceeded in person to the House of
Commons, attended by his guard and desperadoes
that he had for some time entertained at Whitehall, to
the number of three or four hundred, armed with
partizans, sword and pistol,* having previously withdrawn the guard appointed by the members for their
own protection, and refused them any other than
one which they suspected to be exclusively devoted
to himself, and which they had therefore themselves
dismissed.† Entering, with a severe aspect, the
apartment in which the members were assembled,
his attendants waiting without, the House respect-
fully rose, and made a lane for his passage to the
Speaker's chair. He informed them, as soon as he
was seated, that he was come in person to seize the
five members whom his Attorney-general had impeached; but these members had already betaken
themselves to the City for protection. The King
next proceeded to ask the Speaker, who continued
standing below him, if any of the members impli-
cated were in the House? That officer, falling on
his knees, answered: 'I have neither eyes to see, nor
tongue to speak, but as the House is pleased to
direct me, whose servant I am, and I humbly ask
pardon, that I cannot give any other answer to what
your Majesty is pleased to demand of me.' The
King replied, 'I think you are in the right'; adding,

---

* Ludlow.      † Milton.

'Well, since I see all the birds are flown, I do expect from you that you do send them to me as soon as they return hither.' He then departed, several of the members exclaiming as he passed out, 'Privilege, privilege!'* The next day he proceeded to the City and made the same demand of the Council at the Guildhall, but he was heard in silence, and as he retired the populace shouted, 'Privileges of Parliament,' while one individual, approaching the carriage window, exclaimed in a loud voice, 'To your tents, O Israel.'" The reign of violence had begun, and Charles had set the example.†

A strong light is thrown on the state of public feeling in London at this exciting juncture by an

* Thos. Cromwell's *Life of Cromwell.*

† The Speaker of the House of Commons (Mr. Gully, M.P.) in a lecture delivered at Carlisle on the 9th January, 1899, gives an interesting account as to the taking down in shorthand of the King's speech on that occasion :

"John Rushworth, Clerk Assistant of the Long Parliament, and author of *Rushworth's Collections,* was a shorthand writer, and he frequently made notes as he sat at the table of the House. Notice was taken of this, and it was ordered that they should be open to inspection, and should not be taken away. On the 3rd of January, 1642, when the King came to the House with his guards to seize five members whom he wanted to prosecute for high treason for words spoken in debate, his Majesty made a short speech from the Speaker's place, which Rushworth took down in shorthand. The King afterwards sent for Rushworth, and demanded a copy of his speech in the House. Rushworth besought his Majesty to remember that a Yorkshire member had been sent to the Tower for merely telling the King what words had been spoken in the House by another member, to which his Majesty replied, ' I do not ask you to tell me what was said by any member of the House, but what I said myself ' ; whereupon Rushworth gave obedience, transcribed the speech, and gave the transcript to the King, who had it printed and published."

unpublished MS. journal of the son of a member of
the Long Parliament—a King's Counsel—which is
in my possession. The entries are made day by
day, in a pocket almanac for 1641-2, and are
preceded by a memorandum written in a curious
mixture of French, Italian, and English, setting forth
his purpose in writing them, viz., that he might,
from time to time, refresh his memory as to the
occurrences recorded.   On the 1st January, three
days before the King attempted to arrest the five
members, the diarist writes :

"The beginning of this yeare thinges are in a most
distressed state, soe y$^t$ wee cannot w$^{th}$out God's most infinite
Mercy expect any Thing this ensuing yeare but bloody and
tumultuous times.   Y$^e$ Parliament, w$^h$ Committee of y$^e$ house
of Commons sit, this New Yeer's day in Guildhall for some
feeres they have, they have 2 or 3 train bands to guard them.
Thinges are now come to y$^t$ verticall point that wee must of
necessity conceive they cannot hold out as they are one
fortnight longer, w$^{th}$out some revolution or other; the City is
apprehensive of great dangers y$^t$ doe threaten them.   The
house of Commons feare some attemptes upon their persons,
what will be the issue of these thinges is beyond y$^e$ depth of
man's wisdome to fathom ; but I am confident as thinges now
stand noe man will give 2 yeeres purchese for another's life.
If God p'serve me and my friendes in safety till this daye
twelfe-month this particular note in observation may put me
in minde to give thankes to Almighty God and acknowledge
it hath beene only his power and protection hath provided for
our welfare beyonde all our hopes, for in the judgment of man
y$^e$ whole kingdome can scarce subsist soe long without
publicque ruin.   If it please his divine providence yet to
reconcile the King's Majestee and the Parliament w$^{th}$out
much exclusion of good, wee must all acknowledge it is y$^e$
Lorde's work, notwithstanding y$^e$ English nation is noted by
historians to be secure enough in times of greatest danger.
I hope all things will succeed as they desire and believe (who)

never see any danger till they feele it, yet are at this present soe sensible of danger y$^t$ noe night, almost, scapes w$^{th}$out some alarme and men's feares will not afford them quiet enough to rest in their beds.

"There are at this present many men deeply engaged (concerned) on y$^e$ p$^t$ of y$^e$ house of Commons soe y$^t$ if y$^e$ kinges party prevaile they can expect nothinge but destruction soe y$^t$ they will allow of noe agreementes unless theire owne safety is included, there are as many engaged in y$^e$ King and Queene's p$^{t,}$ men of desperate fortunes who must consequently give his Majestie desperate councell and unlesse y$^e$ 2 p'ties come to a very equell poyse, soe y$^t$ they are contente to pardon all on both sides, one side must neede be quite ruined ; but it may pleese God to turne y$^e$ kinges heart to harken to y$^e$ advice of his pliament to grant their reesonable requestes and soe to temper their consultationes y$^t$ they may not require more than hee may w$^{th}$ his honor grant and things possibly may goe well, w$^{ch}$ if they doe wee may only say of our kingdome y$^t$ wee were *Tantum non confuse.*"

"Jan. 3rd.—Some of y$^e$ house of Commons impeached and my Lord Mandeville ; y$^e$ Citty troubled. On y$^e$ 10th y$^e$ kinge went to Hampton Court ; on y$^e$ 11th y$^e$ parliament guarded from Grocers' Hall to Westminster w$^{th}$ much force, by water and by land."

"Jan. 26th.—There hath beene about this time divers attemptes upon Cheapside Crosse, some hurt is done to itt but not very much because many of y$^e$ inhabitants doe stand for it and defend it."

"Mch. 13.—This weeke great expectation of y$^e$ kinges answere from Newmarket. It came on Friday night it was a deniall and on Monday y$^e$ declaration came out."

"May 11.—Lord Mayor committed to y$^e$ Tower."

"July.—On y$^e$ 12th we had a great report y$^t$ Hartford was fired and y$^e$ Cavaliers were there w$^{ch}$ put y$^e$ whole county of Essex into a great feare. Eping Beacon was fired. Theare was a generall watch every where y$^t$ night but y$^e$ news was all false, only a barne was fired by chance. This Mid-

August wee have not heerd anything lately from yᵉ king only a p'clamation proclaiming yᵉ Lord of Essex and all his adhœrents traytores; 'tis generally fered yᵗ yᵉ king endeavours to get a considerable army and then to march uppe for London. My Lord of Essex is daily expected to goe wee know not whither . . . the countyes are generally for the parliament, soe long as they are hastened and encouraged by yᵉ presence of their parliamᵗ men, but as soone as they are gone their heartes faile them."

"The word now is, ' Short shoes and long cornes to yᵉ enemies of olde England."

" Aug. 9th.—I subscribe 20lb at Ongar (to parlᵗ fund)."

" NOTE.—Yᵉ king's colours are Murry or purple and white, the Prince's greene and yᵉ parliamente's orange."

On the 10th January, Charles left Whitehall never to return until he came back to die. On the same day Parliament, including the five members, and escorted by the whole city, reassembled in their Chamber.

In July the first blood was drawn. Funds had to be provided for the Parliamentary Army, and subscriptions (not *forced*) were raised, Cromwell giving £500 and John Hampden £1,000. In August Cromwell seized the Castle of Cambridge, and secured the University plate, worth £20,000, which was being sent to the King. But he refused to allow his old college—Sidney Sussex—to be deprived of its plate.

Here is a curious letter,* in which " *one Mr. Cromwell, a Parliament man,*" is mentioned. It is addressed

> " To his much-esteemed ffrend
>         Mr. Samuel Drake at his
>         ffather's house in Codby (?),
>                 Nigh Hallifax."
> These do

* In the Author's collection.

OLIVER CROMWELL.
From a contemporary miniature by Van Berg (signed)
in the Author's Collection.

"" Honest Dominie,—'Twas my misfortune not only not to receive a letter from you, when (Sir Gifford did) but also not a word of remembrance in his; but I will interpret fairly of your actions, and thinke you were so busied about his maiesties' affayres (for I doubt not you are made some Colonell already) y$^t$ you were forced to neglect your owne, or soe consequently youre ffrendes; or else perhaps being in hot service at Hull (not against S$^r$ John Hotham but against . . . .) you were so wearied out with the siege and battell that you c$^d$ set to do nothing before you had taken y$^r$ rest . . . . to gratifie you you shall know that ours, Trinity Queens and Pembroke this last week sent all theire plate guarded by 30 men with muskets and pistols towardes Yorke, they past Huntingdon safely, but at Stangate how there lay store of men to intercept them, gathered together by y$^e$ *command of one Mr. Cromwell, a Parliament man;* our men (it being night) had like unawares to have marched down, not suspecting any opposition and not seeing the troupes in ambush w$^{ch}$ if they had donne all theire carriage had beene taken away and scarce one of them had escaped with life, but by chance *this Cromwell* rid up y$^e$ hill to see if he c$^d$ spy our men whom he expected y$^t$ night and so betrayed y$^t$ w$^{ch}$ otherwise they had (not?) knowne. They therefore seeing such dangers nighe them returned home safely and delivered y$^e$ plate back. There are many at this time abut y$^e$ neighboring townes as Grancester, Trimpington, &c., up in armes and are shrewdly suspected to watch an opportunity to steale our plate, wherefore at Trinity they watch every night, and on Sunday night our College servants all watch about the College; *the roundheads are still trayning* about us, but I c$^d$ wish as Mr. ffothergill wisht in y$^e$ Chappell when he preacht on Sunday .was sevennight that they w$^d$ leave this trayning and rather trayne themselves up candidly and in good manners. I thinke now you have enough newes from this barren place nay more than you did expect, y$^r$ fruitefull soil cannot but afford more plenty w$^{ch}$ if you will please let me participate you shall oblige y$^r$ truly loving ffreind,

" HIEROME POTKIN

" *Cambridge, August 9th*, 1642.

" Send as soon as you cann."

NOTE.—Cromwell became Col. C. in 1643.—*See* Carlyle, vol. i. p. 170.

In the Journals of the House of Commons under date 15th August, 1642, it is stated that Sir Philip Stapleton gave an account in the House, from the Committee for the Defence of the Kingdom, that " Mr. Cromwell, in Cambridgeshire, had seized the magazine in the Castle at Cambridge, and had hindered the carrying of the plate from that University. And on the 18th August a Committee was appointed to prepare an order for the indemnity of Mr. Cromwell and Mr. Walton, and those that have or shall assist them in the stopping of the plate that was going from Cambridge to York." So, notwithstanding his *faux pas* in going up the hill at the wrong time, Oliver *did* manage to secure the plate, in spite of the vigilant watch kept upon it by the College servants.

# CHAPTER IV.

**Civil War begins, 1642.** The first Civil War began in 1642. On the 22nd August of that year Charles unfurled his standard at Nottingham, "on the evening of a very stormy and tempestuous day." He had an army of 10,000 men, formed of " all sorts and conditions." Retainers of country gentlemen and idlers, and all the ruffians and dissolute fellows that could be mustered from the great towns. But it was led by trained soldiers, men who had received a splendid training in the Dutch and German wars. The Earl of Lindsey, a competent soldier, was appointed Commander-in-Chief—destined, however, soon to find a soldier's grave.

Here Prince Rupert, a dashing young Cavalry officer, makes his *debût*, being appointed General of Cavalry at the age of twenty-three. The estimable Earl of Falkland, so soon to fall at Newbury, one of the gallant Verney family, and many other men who were to make great reputations during the next few years, were with the King.

There can be little question that if the King's army had been composed of soldiers worthy of their commanders—men like Cromwell's 2,000, who were soon to play so memorable a part—there would quickly have been an end to the incipient rebellion. Happily for the cause of liberty it was not so ; for it was formed largely of bands of retainers who

thought much more of their chieftains than of their
King, and of ruffians, soldiers of fortune, whose
thoughts were mainly intent upon loot and rapine.
Moreover the army was utterly undisciplined, its
chiefs jealous of each other, their councils divided,
and the King—untrustworthy himself—trusted no
one about him.

And how was it with the Parliamentary host that
was rapidly gathering around Northampton ?   In
one respect only was it superior to that of the King,
for against his 10,000 men they opposed twice that
number, being commanded by the Earl of Essex,
son of Queen Elizabeth's unfortunate favourite.  This
army was composed of material quite as unfitted for
warlike operations as that of the King.  Its leaders
were vastly inferior to those of the Royal Army, and
its Commander-in-Chief, although perfectly loyal to
the cause, was a dull man, without either initiative to
plan an attack, or resource to retrieve a disaster—
defects soon to be demonstrated in the first great
battle of the war.

Before further referring to that battle, it will be
well to glance at the relative positions of the contending parties at the opening of the great drama.
Frederic Harrison, in his admirable book on
Cromwell,* says, " In wealth, in numbers, and in
cohesion the Parliament was stronger than the King.
To him there had rallied most of the greater nobles,
many of the lesser gentry, some proportion of the
richer citizens, the townsmen of the West, and the
rural population generally of the West and North of
England.

* *Oliver Cromwell* (Macmillan, 1895).

"For the Parliament stood a strong section of the Peers and greater gentry, the great bulk of the lesser gentry, the townsmen of the richer parts of England, the whole Eastern and home counties, and, lastly, the City of London."

As is usual in revolutions, the "classes" were largely with the Court, while the "masses," especially in the great towns, were for Reform; as a rule, the North and West stood for the King, and the East and South for Parliament. But while the contest was waged with varying fortunes in the North and West, the East of England, from the Wash to the Solent, never passed out of the control of Parliament.

**Edgehill, 23rd Oct., 1642.** The Battle of Edgehill in Warwickshire was fought on the 23rd October, 1642. At that time Oliver was Captain of the 67th troop of horse, ·counting sixty sabres, raised and equipped by himself; his brother-in-law, Desborough, being his quarter-master; Cromwell's eldest son, Oliver, was cornet of another troop, while his cousin, John Hampden, was colonel of the 20th regiment of foot.

Essex had been ordered by Parliament to follow the King, and "by battle or other way, rescue him from his perfidious counsellors and restore him to Parliament," but the King out-manœuvred him, and by quick marching opened the way to the capital. Essex hastened after him and came up with the Royal Army on Sunday evening at Edgehill. Every advantage was on the King's side; his position was better and he was superior in numbers, artillery and cavalry. No sooner had the fight commenced, than Sir "Faithful" Fortescue deserted to the King's side with his entire regiment, throwing the Parliamentary forces into disorder.  Rupert was not slow to take advantage of this treachery, and swooping down upon Essex's left wing, drove it off the field into Kineton.  While this was going on, the King's left routed part of Essex's right wing, and he, believing that all was lost, seized a pike and prepared to die at the head of his regiment.

**Rupert the Plunderer.**   But all was not lost, for Rupert's soldiers of fortune took to plundering, and Oliver had yet to be reckoned with.  His troop and twelve others, joining the remnant of Essex's foot, dashed into the King's infantry, destroying regiment after regiment, capturing the Royal Standard that had been so bravely unfurled at Nottingham, and killing the Earl of Lindsey, Charles's Commander-in-Chief.

The King himself narrowly escaped capture, being only saved by the timely return of Rupert from his plundering expedition, as evening was closing in, and he was only able to save the remnants of the Royal Army.  About 4,000 men lay on the bloody field, and the result of the fight was to leave things as they were before, for it was a drawn battle.

" But the moral advantage rested with the King. Essex had learned that his troops were no match for the Cavaliers, and his withdrawal to Warwick left open the road to the capital.

" Rupert  pressed for an instant march on London, but the proposal found stubborn opponents among the moderate Royalists, who dreaded the complete triumph of Charles as much as his defeat."*

* Green's *Short History.*

Charles went on to Oxford, which he caused to be strongly fortified ; here he found a hearty welcome, but did not long remain on this occasion, for his dashing nephew Rupert had captured Reading and Brentford, within striking distance of London.

In the meantime Essex had reached the capital, where the panic had already subsided, and being joined by the City trainbands, Charles was forced back upon his Oxford quarters.

But this first trial of the opposing forces brought out into strong relief the radical faults of both, the unsteadiness of the Parliamentary foot soldiers contrasting strongly with the splendid qualities of the Puritan horse from Oliver's Eastern counties. It also showed the disorganisation of the King's command, his weakness in infantry, and the dangerous recklessness of Rupert—a recklessness which was destined to be of good service to the Parliamentary cause on many a field yet to be fought. Cromwell, born soldier as he was, was quick to note all these things, and to turn them to good account.

Richard Baxter. "At Alcester, twenty miles away, Richard Baxter was preaching on that eventful Sunday from the text, 'The Kingdom of Heaven suffereth violence,' little knowing what was doing at Edgehill, while his audience distinctly heard the solemn booming of the cannon during the whole of his discourse."*

[In Carlyle's *Letters and Speeches* (ed. 1897, vol. ii. p. 136) is a letter, dated 17th March, 1642-3, from " John Cory, Merchant of Norwich," giving an account of a successful raid upon

* Timmins's *History of Warwickshire.*

Lowestoft, by Col. Cromwell, Oliver having heard of a meeting of Malignants there. I have in my possession a small book, a *Life of Oliver Cromwell*, in which are some MS. notes respecting a certain Capt. H. Squire, made by some of his relatives. Amongst the rest is a copy of a letter respecting Cromwell's attack upon Lowestoft. It is addressed :

"For Capt. H. Squire,
"at his quarters, Oundle.

"Dear friend,—We have secret and sure hints that a meeting of the malignants takes place at Lowestoft in Co. Suffolk on Tuesday. Now, I want your ayd, so come with all speed on getting this, with your troop, and tell no one your route, but lett me see you ere sundown.

"From your friend and commandant,
"O. Cromwell."

The book contains two water-colour portraits of Capt. Squire, showing the red coat. In a note it says: "This H. Squire lived at Thrapstone and Oundle, also Yaxley, where he joined a Stilton troop, 1641, and was cornet and rode as lieutenant at Naseby, where he was wounded, and fought all through the Civil War, but gave up when they killed the King, and so never had any more to do with them. In his memorandum and history which he left, much now remains, but very rotten. I have a copy of some parts but it is not connected, as it had been mixed and torn in removals, and laid up got damp and rotten. He died about 1690 or 1692 uncertain, and he is buried at Yaxley, I believe, or else Thrapstone ; he was a merchant, and so has the family been for centuries at Thrapstone, Oundle, Peterboro' and Lynn."

Evidently a portion of the "Squire" correspondence dealt with by Carlyle in vol. ii., *Letters and Speeches*. The hand-writing in these Notes is clearly that of the beginning of the 18th century, so that the letters, etc., must have been in existence at that date, and could not have been forged by Carlyle's correspondent. They are however very much too doubtful in character to be accepted as genuine.]

Fifteen years after Edgehill, the Protector, in relating to his second Parliament a conversation

he had with John Hampden about this time,
described the kind of men he had been careful to
enlist into his Puritan regiments. He said, " I had a
very worthy Friend then, and he was a very noble
person, and I know his memory is very grateful to
all—Mr. John Hampden. At my first going out into
this engagement, I saw our men were beaten at every
hand. ' Your troops,' said I, ' are most of them old
decayed serving-men, and tapsters, and such kind of
fellows ; and,' said I, ' their troops are gentlemen's
sons ; younger sons and persons of quality ; do you
think that the spirits of such base mean fellows will
ever be able to encounter gentlemen that have
honour and courage and resolution in them ? '
Truly, I did represent to him in this manner, con-
scientiously and truly I did tell him : ' You must get
men of a spirit ; and take it not ill what I say,—I
know you will not,—of a spirit that is likely to go on
as far as gentlemen will go ; or else you will be
beaten still.' I told him so ; I did truly. He was a
wise and worthy person, and he did think that I
talked a good notion, but an impracticable one. I
raised such men as had the fear of God before them,
as made some conscience of what they did ; and
from that day forward, I must say to you, they were
never beaten, and wherever they were engaged
against the enemy, they beat continually."

Here is Bulstrode Whitelocke's description of
Oliver's men : " He had a brave regiment of horse of
his countrymen, most of them freeholders and freeholders' sons, and who upon matter of conscience
engaged in this quarrel, and under Cromwell. And
thus, being well armed within by the satisfaction of

their own consciences, and without by good iron armour, they would as one man stand firmly and charge desperately."

Cromwell obtained his knowledge of the art of war from Captain John Dalbier, a veteran of Dutch extraction, who had seen much service abroad. Oliver was diligent in the drilling of his troopers, and in teaching them how to handle their weapons, and to manage their horses. "As an officer," says Waller, " he was obedient, and did never dispute my orders, or argue upon them."*

"Colonel" Cromwell, 1643. By May in the following year, Oliver's "troop of horse" had swelled to 2,000 men, and he had become "Colonel" Cromwell, and this is how he was described in a "news-letter" of that period : "As for Colonel Cromwell, he hath 2,000 brave men, well disciplined ; no man swears but he pays his twelve pence ; if he be drunk, he is set in the stocks, or worse ; if one calls the other Roundhead, he is cashiered ; insomuch that the countries where they come leap for joy of them, and come in and join with them. Happy were it if all the forces were thus disciplined."

On the 13th of May, 1643, Cromwell won the first fight where he was in chief command. Outside Grantham he met a body of Cavaliers who had been carrying all before them for months, and although they were double his number he completely routed them and cut them in pieces. His men had only

* Captain Dalbier. This most capable officer becoming dissatisfied with the Parliamentary cause, deserted to the King, and in a fight near Kingston-on-Thames was slain by Oliver's men.

been in arms nine months, but they were already seasoned cavalry.

This small success of Cromwell's gave but a flickering gleam of hope to the Parliament, for everywhere the Royal Army was steadily gaining ground, and now one of the heaviest blows the popular cause had yet to receive was to come from remote Cornwall. The vast majority of Cornishmen had always been loyal to the Crown, although there had not been wanting men, even in Elizabeth's reign, who dared to speak their minds in opposition, for when, in 1575, that Queen sent a message to Parliament commanding it not to meddle in the matter of religion, and directing the Commons to leave all such matters to the initiative of the clergy, Peter Wentworth, member for Tregony, spoke out in unmistakeable language. He plainly told the Queen that she was subject to the law, and that without free speech it was a scorn and a mockery to call them a " Parliament," and then he filled up the measure of offence against her Imperious Majesty by adding, " There was none without fault, no, not even their noble Queen," and joyfully went to prison in attestation of his sincerity.

Down to a period long subsequent to that of the Civil Wars Cornwall was almost as remote as the Hebrides from the general life of the nation. Its peninsular position, its dissimilarity of language, and the Celtic devotion of its people to their local chieftains, all tended to cause them to subordinate their personal opinions to those of their leaders, and the latter were almost uniformly strongly Royalist in sentiment.

In this month Lord Stamford, the commander of the Parliamentary forces, determined to try his fortune in Cornwall, and with a strong force **Battle of Stratton (Launceston), May, 1643.** marched upon Launceston; but being met by Sir Bevil Grenville, who was in command of a small force, the Parliamentarians were defeated, with the loss of 2,000 men and all their ordnance. Lord Stamford then made a hurried retreat, being followed by the Royalists, under Sir Ralph Hopton, through Devonshire and Somersetshire, when they were finally defeated on Lansdowne Hill, near Bath. In this battle Hopton was dangerously wounded, and Sir Bevil Grenville killed.

In the following year Essex entered Cornwall, being closely followed by the King, and in July the army of the Parliament was totally defeated by him at Lostwithiel, the foot soldiers being taken prisoners, Essex and other leaders escaping by sea from Fowey.

**Oliver in Cornwall, 1646.** It is not generally known that Cromwell took part in Fairfax's campaign in Cornwall. On February 25, 1646, he was present at the capture of Launceston, and accompanied Fairfax in his victorious march through the county.

"The Royalist forces in Cornwall were speedily brought to a surrender; Goring fled to France, Hopton agreed to a treaty by which his troops were disbanded, and on March 21 Fairfax began his return from Truro. Four days later he and Cromwell went on to Plymouth." *

* *Launceston, Past and Present*, by Alfred E. Robbins.

JOHN HAMPDEN.

From a miniature in monochrome by Pettitot, in the Author's Collection.

A cruel blow was now to fall upon Cromwell and the Parliamentary cause. Lord Essex's "masterly inactivity" was daily becoming more pronounced, and he rarely fought unless it was impossible to avoid doing so. His army lay in Buckinghamshire, was very badly officered, and under lax discipline. This becoming known to Prince Rupert, who was at Oxford, that officer determined to make a sudden raid upon the Parliamentary forces, and coming up with a small company under the command of John Hampden, on Chalgrove Field, he easily defeated them.

**Cbalgrove, June, 1643.**

Hampden was mortally wounded, and to the consternation of his men was seen riding off the field before the fight had ended, " which he never used to do " ; he died a few days after, his last words being, " Save my bleeding country." *

* " Julie 1. This daie there is gone from Thame 4,000 soldiers : 2,000 to Ethrop (?) to be quartered, 2,000 to meet Prince Rupert's hignes towards Bucks : they have taken away some 2 drakes to every Regiment, my L. G. sticks close to Thame, and if I am not mistaken in *phisnognomie* he loves to have no harme, but to be quiet if he might, for haveinge well viewed his noble person, I judge he loves sleepe ? good diet ? and ease, or else I am much mistaken in my skill. At Grendon the works lie still, at Tetsworth there lies about 700 dragoons w^ch weare under the commands of Colonell Miles : whoe uppon some dislike, hath laide downe his commission and is gone from them, their sergant maiour is sicke and there is no commander to leade them : but sometimes our Captaine Middleton leads them uppon anie designe ; my opinion is they be lazlie and leave it to betr judgment."— *From a contemporary MS. in the Author's collection.*

On comparing this account with Green's *History of the English People,* vol. iii. p. 222 (1882), it is clear that the

Hampden's refusal to pay ship money—on the
ground of its being an unconstitutional tax, having
been ordered on the King's authority only—was one
of the proximate causes of the war. Oliver, whose
accession to the highest position in the State had
been early foretold by Hampden, deeply felt the
loss of his cousin.

---

year is 1643, and that the letter was written just one week
after the death of John Hampden, on Chalgrove Field.

The anonymous writer's description of the Lord General
(Lord Essex) is very characteristic, and true to the letter.

## CHAPTER V.

**Panic in Parliament.**  " Disaster followed disaster. Essex, more and more anxious for a peace, fell back on Uxbridge, while a cowardly surrender of Bristol to Prince Rupert, gave Charles the second city of the kingdom and the mastery of the West. The news fell on the Parliament like a sentence of death." The Lords debated nothing but proposals of peace. London itself was divided ; "a great multitude of the wives of substantial citizens" clamoured at the door of the Commons for peace ; and a flight of six of the few peers who remained at Westminster to the camp at Oxford, proved the general despair of the Parliament's success.

From this moment, however, the firmness of the Parliamentary leaders began slowly to reverse the fortunes of the war. If Hampden was gone, Pym remained. The spirit of the Commons was worthy of their great leader, and Waller was received on his return from his defeat on Roundway Hill "as if he had brought the King prisoner with him." *

The great and pressing danger of the moment was the existence of a strong army in the North under

* Green's *Short History*.

75

Newcastle, and the Commons prepared resolutely to meet it. The Fairfaxes were shut up in Hull, and in some danger there, so it was resolved to make a great effort to secure the line of the Trent, with Lincoln and Newark. Cromwell pushed on to

**Gainsborough Fight, 28th July, 1643.** the relief of Gainsborough, having several severe skirmishes on the way. On the 28th July, after a forced march of fifty-five miles, he came up with the young General Cavendish, who, with a strong force of horse, was posted on a hill a couple of miles outside Gainsborough. Here is Oliver's description of the fight : "We came up horse to horse, where we disputed it with our swords and pistols a pretty time, all keeping close order, so that one could not break through the other. At last, they a little shrinking, our men perceiving it pressed in upon them, and immediately routed this whole body, some flying on the one side, and others on the other of the enemy's reserve, and our men pursuing them, had chase and execution about five or six miles." Cavendish had a regiment in reserve, with which he intended falling on Oliver's rear, but to his great surprise he was himself charged and, with his men, forced into a quagmire from which few escaped, Cavendish himself being killed. " My Captain-Lieutenant (Berry) slew him with a thrust under his short ribs."

Gainsborough was relieved, but a much greater danger confronted Cromwell ; he presently found himself in front of Newcastle's main army, which was vastly superior to his own. "The peril was extreme ; the footmen from Gainsborough were driven in, but Cromwell divided his troops into two parties, causing them to retreat in turns, facing the enemy's fresh horse; and at length, by nine removes, he drew off his whole command, all exhausted as it was, from before Newcastle's army, with the loss of only two men. For the second time Cromwell's troopers had utterly routed the Cavalier squadrons in a fair charge. But this last combat proved much more. It had shown, in one of the most difficult operations in war (a small body of horse holding an army in check, whilst its own infantry retreats), unfaltering discipline in the men, and masterly tactics in their handling. This affair is the first glimpse we obtain of really scientific war. The Ironsides were now led by a consummate general of horse. 'This,' wrote Whitelocke, 'was the beginning of his great fortunes, and he now began to appear in the world.'" *

The Royal successes continued in the West, Rupert's brother securing Devonshire for the King. Gloucester too was on the point of falling, being reduced to its last barrel of powder, but the timely arrival of Essex compelled Charles to raise the siege.

From Gloucester Essex marched back to London, fighting the first battle of Newbury on the way. Here the gallant and amiable Lord Falkland fell, crying, " Peace, Peace ! " The battle was indecisive, although Rupert made desperate efforts, but the London trainbands were too much for him.

Alliance with Scotland. The balance between the two parties was now practically even, and some decisive action was needed to cause it to

* F. Harrison.

incline to one side or the other. For the King, nothing but a great victory would serve, but the Parliament had another "string to its bow." Charles, by the aid of his evil genius, Laud, having alienated the Scotch by his attacks on their system of public worship, Parliament determined to make a close alliance with them. They despatched Sir Harry Vane to arrange a Treaty, which he quickly accomplished, but the price that England had to pay for the help of the Scotch was a very heavy and burdensome one, being nothing less than the imposition of the Presbyterian formulary upon the whole country. "Unity in religion" was demanded, and the "Unity" was to be Presbyterian ; tender consciences were to be strained, and a rigorous system, scarcely less onerous than that from which the country had suffered so severely under Laud, was to be established.

But there was no help for it, although Cromwell, an Independent of Independents, detested the condition, and Pym and most of the other leaders in Parliament were still moderate Episcopalians. With his usual fatuity at critical moments, Charles caused all hesitation to disappear by making arrangements for an invasion of Scotland by Irish Catholics.

The Covenant, 15th Sept., 1643.        The mere rumour of his intention to import Irish rebels whose hands were still red with the blood of massacred Protestants, caused intense dissatisfaction amongst his own supporters, and many of his officers threw up their commissions ; the peers who had recently fled from London returned to the Parliament, and the incipient Royalist reaction there, disappeared.

**Scots in England, Jan., 1644.** Pym, the most consummate statesman of his time, died in December, 1643, but his vast plans had been sufficiently matured to enable Parliament to arm fifty thousand men. In January, a Scotch army of 20,000 men crossed the border "in a great frost and snow," compelling the Earl of Newcastle to march north to meet it. In February, Cromwell made a transient reappearance in Parliament, resulting in his appointment as lieutenant-general under Manchester, with an army of 14,000 men, and with orders to co-operate with Sir Thomas Fairfax in Yorkshire. The latter general being relieved of the presence of Newcastle, marched against the English troops from Ireland which had landed at Chester, and having destroyed them, returned to Yorkshire to besiege Selby.

It was becoming increasingly evident that Yorkshire was soon to become the theatre of important and probably decisive events. The Earl of Newcastle, leaving the Scots army at Durham, hastened back to York, where he was besieged by Fairfax and the Scots army which had quickly followed him. Thither also marched Manchester, with Cromwell and his 14,000 men, "mostly Puritans," while Essex and Waller proceeded against Charles at Oxford, closely investing that city.

In the meantime Rupert had left Oxford to effect a diversion in favour of Newcastle, and having recruited his army on the Welsh border, by a bold and clever movement evaded the Parliamentary armies in Yorkshire and threw himself into York with 20,000 men. The Parliamentary generals, hearing of the approach of Rupert, had raised the siege and placed their armies in position on Marston Moor, but he avoided them by crossing the river.

**Marston Moor, 2nd July, 1644.** Newcastle was satisfied with the present success of the Royal arms, but Rupert insisted on his joining him in a set battle on the morrow.

Marston Moor, eight miles out from York, was fought on the 2nd July, 1644, and here is a character-istic engraving of an incident in that fight. A troop of pikemen are marching along a road in a hollow, whilst their Captain, in advance of them, is giving out a psalm. The men's faces are turned upwards towards a stern-looking figure on horseback, who is slowly marching along a bank above them. It is Oliver, and well it is for them and for the Parliamentary cause that he is there on that fateful day, for, but for his presence, his bravery and wonderful genius, the tyrant's forces would have gained a decisive victory.

" The day was dull and thunderous, with occasional showers ; and it was far into the afternoon before the two armies were in position. Hour after hour they stood on the moor glaring at each other across the ditch which parted them, each watching his opportunity to attack."*

Rupert, with his usual recklessness, was for attacking at once, but was restrained by his seniors ;—he was not to wait long, however, before his " lust for battle " was more than satisfied.

Evidently the Royal Generals had not yet awoke to a full conception of the character of the man who was so soon to " scatter them before him like a little dust," for, strange to relate, at seven o'clock on this

* F. Harrison.

BATTLE OF MARSTON MOOR.

July evening, thinking there would be no fighting
till morning, they retired to rest !

Scarcely had they been comfortably settled for the
night, when Oliver, who commanded the left wing,
composed of his trusted men from the Eastern
counties—horse and foot,—suddenly fell on Rupert,
(who was opposite to him), dashing into his chosen
regiment, scattering it like chaff, and receiving a
wound which only caused him to exclaim, "*A miss
is as good as a mile.*"

There is a spirited picture showing Oliver, his
arm in a sling in the thick of a desperate charge,
directing and animating all around him.   How like
the sturdy rebel that he was, that he should thus
rudely disturb the enemy in their first sleep !

Having scattered Rupert's men, and permitted
his foremost lines to pursue them to the very gates
of York, Oliver was not likely to follow that
commander's example at Edgehill, by following up
his own success regardless of what was going on
in other parts of the field.   Halting his main force,
he paused to see how matters sped on his right,
and it was well that he did so, for confusion and
defeat reigned supreme.   The Scotch Commander,
"believing all was lost, fled towards Leeds, while
Fairfax and Manchester were swept away in the
melée."

This was the opportunity for the genius of
Cromwell to assert itself.   Victory had to be plucked
out of defeat, and he was just the man to accomplish
it.   The generals of both the opposing armies were
in full flight to opposite points of the compass, each
side thinking the cause lost.   Oliver, with a soldier's

eye, promptly taking in the situation, rallied his men after his victorious charge against Rupert, and in an hour, according to Frederic Harrison's graphic account, his genius "had changed defeat into victory. Launching the Scotch troopers of his own wing against Newcastle's Whitecoats, and sending the infantry of the Eastern Association to succour the remnants of the Scots in the centre, he swooped with the bulk of his own cavalry round the rear of the King's army, and fell upon Goring's victorious troopers on the opposite side of the field. Taking them in the rear, all disordered as they were in the chase and the plunder, he utterly crushed and dispersed them. Having thus with his own squadron annihilated the cavalry of both the enemy's wings, he closed round upon the Royalist centre, and there the Whitecoats and the remnants of the King's infantry were cut to pieces almost to a man." With this brilliant action, the victory of Marston Moor—giving York and the whole North of England to the Parliament—was complete. Newcastle fled over sea ; and Rupert, with six thousand horse at his back, rode southward to Oxford.

It was here that Rupert, having tasted the quality of Oliver's men, first called them "*Ironsides*."

But the effect of this great victory was neutralised in the South-west by the jealousies of the leaders and the feebleness and wretched policy that directed the war there, and by September, 1644, the Parliament had no army in the South-west. Cromwell could not be in two places at the same time, but he was continually urging Parliament to take such measures as should end this confusion, or, he said, "we

shall speedily be undone." By dint of great
exertions an army was got together again, and
on Sunday, the 29th October, the
second battle of Newbury was fought.
The Parliamentary army was superior
in numbers, was well led and fought
well ; but in spite of all, the King was allowed
to draw off his army and artillery, and the
fighting was all in vain. It had become apparent
that noble lords were out of place as leaders of
rebellion against monarchy; Manchester and Essex
had already clearly shown that they had gone
far enough and did not intend to defeat the
King. But Cromwell and his Ironsides had not left
their farms and families merely to make a demons-
tration—they were venturing their lives and their
all, in order to secure civil and religious liberty,
and so Cromwell determined to put an end to
all doubt and vacillation. From his place in
Parliament he denounced Manchester and charged
him with neglecting to follow up advantages gained
in battle, and with desiring to save the King from
defeat.

Cromwell's speech, on the alarming condition into
which the country had fallen through the lack of
earnestness of the Generals, was delivered under
very impressive circumstances. It was a critical
moment ; "there was general silence for a good
space of time." At length he said : "It is now a
time to speak, or for ever hold the tongue. The
important occasion now, is no less than to save a
nation out of a bleeding, nay, almost dying condition, which the long continuance of this war hath

*Second Battle
of Newbury,
29th Oct.,
1644.*

already brought it into; so that without a more speedy, vigorous, and effectual prosecution of the war; —casting off all lingering proceedings like soldiers of fortune, beyond sea, to spin out a war,—we shall make the kingdom weary of us, and hate the name of a Parliament. For what do the enemy say? Nay, what do many say who were friends of Parliament at the beginning? Even this, that the Members of both houses have got great places and commands, and the sword into their hands; and, what by interest in Parliament, what by power in the Army, will perpetually continue themselves in grandeur, and not permit the war speedily to end, lest their own power should determine with it. . . . Therefore, waiving a strict enquiry into the causes of these things, let us apply ourselves to the remedy, which is most necessary. And I hope we have such true English hearts, and zealous affections towards the general weal of our Mother Country, as no Members of either House will scruple to deny themselves, and their own private interests, for the public good; nor account it to be a dishonour done to them, whatever the Parliament shall resolve upon in this weighty matter."

Some of Oliver's speeches have been described as roundabout, involved and vague, but there is a directness about this like one of his own cavalry charges, and it was as effective.

Self=denying Ordinance, 3rd April, 1645.

Before the end of the year the Self-denying Ordinance was passed, by which every Member of Parliament— Lords and Commons—was required to resign his command; and within two months more the army was re-organised on the new model, by which the three armies of Militia and loose levies, under separate authorities, raised for a short time, were consolidated into one standing army of 22,000 men. Sir Thomas Fairfax was appointed to the chief command, but Oliver was the ruling spirit. "The voice was the voice of Fairfax, but the hands were the hands of Oliver."

One of the most interesting relics of the times is Fairfax's Staff of Office, presented to him by Parliament on his appointment as Commander-in-Chief of the famous "New Model" Army. This Staff, which is now in my possession, is made of ebony; it is fifty-four inches in height, and has a silver head, on the top of which the Fairfax arms are engraved. Round the neck is engraved this legend :

MANUS HÆC INIMICA TYRANNIS ENSE

PETIT PLACIDAM SUB LIBERTATE QUIETEM

and around the ferrule

HASTA INPENTORIS ILLUSTRISSIMI

THOMÆ DOMINE FAIRFAX. Anno Dom: 1645
On the top of the silver knob are the Fairfax arms, with the motto

FARE FAC.

The inscription, freely translated, reads :

"The hand hostile to Tyranny sought by the Sword tranquil Peace under Liberty."

"The staff (spear) of the Illustrious Commander, Thomas, Lord Fairfax, Anno Domini, 1645."

Cromwell, being a Member of Parliament, was one of the officers who would have to lay down his command. Would he do it? and if so, what would become of the army, by whom he was idolised? In any event there was work for him to do before the date fixed for the "Self-denial." For a long time past the West was the cause of great anxiety to Parliament, and General Goring and Sir Richard Grenville were in considerable force in Somersetshire. Cromwell was ordered to proceed against Goring, but with an exaggerated notion of his powers, Parliament furnished him with an inadequate force for the service, and, writing from Salisbury on the 9th April, 1645, he beseeches Fairfax to "send what horse and foot you can spare . . . with what convenient expedition may be."

The expedition was entirely successful; Prince Rupert, who was in the neighbourhood, retiring without again trying conclusions with Oliver, the memory of Marston Moor being, doubtless, sufficiently vivid.

Rupert was next heard of at Worcester, from which place he had sent 2,000 troops to Oxford to convoy the King and his ordnance to the former city. This convoy was ordered by the Committee of both Kingdoms to be attacked. "The charge of this service they recommended particularly to General Cromwell, who, looking on himself now as discharged of military employment by the New Ordinance, which was to take effect within a few days, and to have no longer opportunity to serve his country in that way, was, the night before, come to Windsor, from his service in the West, to kiss the General's hand and take leave of him; when, in the morning, ere he was come forth of his chamber, those commands, than which he thought of nothing

CHARLES I.

A CRYPTOGRAM (see Addenda).

From the original, in the Author's Collection.

less in all the world, came to him from the Committee of both Kingdoms." *

Cromwell lost no time—he never did—in getting into Oxfordshire, and on the 24th April, 1645, came up with the convoy at Islip Bridge and utterly routed it, thus defeating Rupert's little design. Some of the flying Royalists took refuge in a strong house in Bletchington, where one Colonel Windebank was in command. Oliver demanded the surrender of this place, and at midnight, his terms having been agreed to, the garrison marched out, leaving the victor some hundreds of muskets and other arms, and seventy-one horses. Poor Windebank went to Oxford, where he was at once court-martialed, so enraged were his party, as Oliver was without foot soldiers and battering guns when he demanded the surrender. It appears that it was the presence of Windebank's young wife in the house, and of other " ladies on a visit there," that caused him to yield without fighting, so " he set his back to the wall of Merton College and received his death-volley with a soldier's stoicism." †

**A Reverse for Oliver, 29 April, 1645.** On the 29th April, Cromwell met with one of his rare reverses, for after summoning the Governor of Farringdon to surrender, without result, he stormed the place with a loss of fourteen men, and then had to draw off his forces discomfited.

In June, Cromwell had not resumed his Parliamentary duties since the passing of the Self-denying Ordinance, for after the affair at Farringdon he had been called away to the Fen Country, which was in

* Sprigge's *Anglia Rediviva*, 1647.   † Heath's *Chronicle*.

a very unsatisfactory state. Says Carlyle: "To Fairfax and his officers, to the Parliament, to the Committee of both Kingdoms, to all persons, it is clear that Cromwell cannot be dispensed with. Fairfax and the Officers petition Parliament that he may be appointed their Lieutenant-General, Commander-in-Chief of the Horse. There is a clear necessity in it. Parliament—the Commons somewhat more readily than the Lords—continue by instalments of 'forty days,' of 'three months,' his services in the Army ; and at length grow to regard him as a constant element there."

A few others got similar leave of absence—similar dispensation from the Self-denying Ordinance. Sprigge's words, already cited, are no doubt veracious; yet there is trace of evidence that Cromwell's continuance in the Army had, even by the framers of the Self-denying Ordinance, been considered a thing possible, a thing desirable. As it well might. To Cromwell himself there was no overpowering felicity in going out to be shot at, except when wanted ; he very probably, as Sprigge intimates, "did let the matter in silence take its own course."

The end of the first Civil War was now well in sight. Fairfax, in a half-hearted way, was threatening Oxford, still held for the King, while Charles was roaming about the Midlands with that cheerful optimism which distinguished him, occasionally engaging in a hunt, at other times driving the cattle of the disaffected before him. On the **Storming of Leicester, 31st May, 1645.** 31st of May, 1645, he stormed and captured Leicester with terrible loss of life to the defenders and immense destruction of property. Oliver had gone into the Fen Country early in June, where he found affairs in "a very ill posture," and had exerted himself, not without success, in effecting an improvement.

But it was becoming evident that Charles was preparing to try his fortune against Oliver's redoubtable Eastern Association.

In a letter dated "Cambridge, 6th June, 1645," and addressed to the authorities of the County Suffolk, Oliver (with others) pleads earnestly for as many horse and foot as they can get together, and as promptly as possible, for "the cloud of the enemy's army hanging still upon the borders, and drawing towards Harborough, make some supposals that they aim at the Association." He complains that "the Army (Fairfax) about Oxford was not yesterday advanced, albeit it was ordered so to do." A place of rendezvous was appointed for the expected reinforcements, and arrangements made for keeping a sharp look-out for Charles. The troops were to have a week's pay in advance, and, incidentally, the rate is mentioned, viz., 14s. a week for a trooper, and 10s. 6d. per week for a dragoon ;—equal to three times these amounts at the present day. Urgent letters were also sent to Fairfax entreating him to come to their help. All came, and not a day too soon !

# CHAPTER VI.

"It was about the noon
Of a glorious day in June,"

in 1645, that the final battle of the first Civil War
was fought, at Naseby. Cromwell and Fairfax had
under their command 10,000 sea-
soned troops, of whom 6,000 were
Cromwell's Ironsides, who had never
known defeat. The King's Army was about equal
in number, and his best Generals were with him,
Rupert, as usual, leading the Cavalry.

The Battle of Naseby, 14th June, 1645.

Here is Carlyle's sketch of this great and decisive
battle :

"The old hamlet of Naseby stands yet, on its old
hill-top, very much as it did in Saxon days, on the
north-western border of Northamptonshire, some
seven or eight miles from Market Harborough in
Leicestershire ; nearly on a line, and nearly midway
between that town and Daventry. A peaceable old
hamlet, of some 800 souls ; clay cottages for
labourers, but neatly thatched and swept ; smith's
shop, saddler's shop, beer-shop, all in order ; forming
a kind of square, which leads off southwards into
two long streets ; the old Church, with its graves,
stands in the centre, the truncated spire finishing
itself with a strange old ball, held up by rods, a
'hollow copper ball which came from Boulogne in

Henry VIII's time.' The ground is upland, moor-
land, though now growing corn ; was not enclosed
till the last generation, and is still somewhat bare
of wood. It stands nearly in the heart of England.
. . . Avon Well, the distinct source of Shakespeare's Avon, is on the western slope of the high
grounds ; Nen and Welland, streams leading towards
Cromwell's Fen Country, begin to gather themselves
from boggy places on the eastern side. The grounds,
as we say, lie high ; and are still known by the
name of 'hills' ; 'Rutput Hill,' 'Mill Hill,' and
'Dust Hill,' precisely as in Rushworth's time. . . .
It was on this high moor-ground, in the centre of
England, that King Charles, on the 14th of June,
1645, fought his last battle ; dashed fiercely against
the New Model Army, which he had despised till
then, and saw himself shivered utterly to ruin thereby.
'Prince Rupert, on the King's right wing, charged
up the hill and carried all before him' ; but Lieutenant-General Cromwell charged downhill on the
other wing, likewise carrying all before him, and did
not gallop off the field to plunder. (Rupert, like the
German mercenary he was, could never keep to
his work when there was a chance of plunder.)

"Cromwell, ordered thither by the Parliament,
had arrived from the Association two days before,
'amid shouts from the whole army' ; he had the
ordering of the horse this morning. Prince Rupert,
on returning from his plunder, finds the King's
Infantry in ruin ; prepared to charge again with the
rallied Cavalry."

"One charge more, gentlemen, and the day is
ours," said Charles ; but his troopers had had enough,

and "broke all asunder," never to reassemble more.
" The chase went through Harborough, where the
King had already been that morning, when, in an
evil hour, he turned back to revenge ' some surprise
of an outpost at Naseby the night before,' and give
the Roundheads battle.

" The Parliamentary Army stood ranged on the
height still partly called Mill Hill, a mile and a half
from Naseby ; the King's Army on a parallel ' hill,'
its back to Harborough ; with the wide table of
upland now called Broad Moor between them ;
where, indeed, the main brunt of the action still
clearly enough shows itself to have been.   There are
hollow spots of a rank vegetation scattered over that
Broad Moor, which are understood to have once
been burial mounds, some of which—one to my
knowledge—have been (with more or less of sacrilege)
verified as such.   A friend of mine has in his cabinet
two ancient grinder-teeth, dug lately from that
ground, and waits for an opportunity to re-bury
them there.    Sound, effectual grinders, one of
them very large, which ate their breakfast on the 14th
morning of June, two hundred years ago, and except
to be clenched once in grim battle, had never work
to do more." *

Rushworth, the historian, Fairfax's Secretary, being
a non-combatant, stayed with the baggage-train near
to Naseby village, about a mile from the scene of the
action.   Here is an extract from a letter, dated two

---

* Relics of the fight are continually turning up in ploughing
season.   A year or two ago a farmer found a sixpence of
Charles I. in the clay as he was ploughing, and it is now in
the Author's collection.

OLIVER CROMWELL.

From a miniature in monochrome by Pettitot in the Author's Collection.

o'clock in the morning of the 15th June, which he addressed to a newspaper :

"A party of theirs, that broke through the left wing of horse, came quite behind the rear to our train ; the leader of them being a person somewhat in habit like the General, in a red montero, as the General had. He came as a friend ; our Commander of the guard of the train went with his hat in his hand, and asked him how the day went ? thinking it had been the General. The cavalier, who we since heard was Rupert, asked him and the rest if they would have quarter. They cried 'No,' gave fire, and instantly beat them off. It was a happy deliverance."

And so Rupert the Plunderer was disappointed once more.

Amongst the prisoners were a number of "ladies of quality in carriages," and above a hundred Irish ladies, not of quality, tattery camp-followers, "with long skean-knives, about a foot in length," which they well knew how to use. . . . "The King's carriage was also taken, with a cabinet and many Royal autographs in it, which when printed made a sad impression against his Majesty—gave, in fact, a most melancholy view of the veracity of his Majesty, ' On the word of a King '—All was lost ! "

Here is Oliver's report to Speaker Lenthall :

"Harborough, 14th June, 1645.

**Oliver to Parliament.** "SIR,—Being commanded by you to this service, I think myself bound to acquaint you with the good hand of God towards you and us. We marched yesterday after the King, who went before us from Daventry to Harborough, and quartered about six miles from him. This day

we marched towards him.   He drew out to meet us;
both armies engaged.   We, after three hours fight
very doubtful, at last routed his army; killed and
took about 5,000; very many officers, but of what
quality we yet know not.   We took also about 200
carriages, all he had, and all his guns, being twelve
in number, whereof two were demi-cannon, two
demi-culverins, and I think the rest sackers.   We
pursued the enemy from three miles short of Harborough to nine beyond, even to the sight of
Leicester, whither the King fled.

"Sir, this is none other but the hand of God; and
to Him alone belongs the glory, wherein none are to
share with Him.   The General (Fairfax) served you
with all faithfulness and honour; and the best com-
mendation I can give him is, that I dare say he
attributes all to God, and wd. rather perish than
assume to himself.

"Which is an honest and a thriving way; and yet
as much for bravery may be given to him in this
action as to a man.   Honest men served you faithfully in this action.   Sir, they are trusty; I beseech
you in the name of God not to discourage them.   I
wish this action may beget thankfulness and humility
in all that are concerned in it.   He that ventures his
life for the liberty of his Country, I wish he trust
God for the liberty of his conscience, and you for
the liberty he fights for.   In this he rests, who is
your most humble servant,

"OLIVER CROMWELL." *

* " Naseby " was fought 14th June, 1645.   In the Author's
collection are some original documents, being orders for
delivery of Munitions of War, etc., to various commanders, in

Cromwell, who hated persecution and the forcing of conscience, seized the opportunity, in announcing the great victory to Parliament, to earnestly plead for those soldiers who were unable to take the Covenant, "honest men who served you faithfully." He pointed out that these men had fought for the liberty of their country, and he expected no less than that Parliament, in accepting their services, would see to it that they should have that liberty—the liberty of conscience—for which they had risked their lives.

But the Presbyterian Church — like all State Churches—in persecuting those who could not accept their system, thought they were rendering God service.

**The Clubmen, 1645.** One of the curious results of the Civil War was the rise of a third party, mainly inhabitants of Wiltshire and portions of the surrounding counties—these were the Clubmen, so called because they were, at first, armed with clubs. Their professed object in banding together was to preserve their property from both parties to

one of which Cromwell's name is mentioned under date 7th May, 1645, five weeks before the Battle of Naseby. It runs thus :

"Delivered y$^e$ day and yeere abovesaid out of his M$^{ts}$ Stoares within y$^e$ office of y$^e$ ordnance unto Capt. Adam Lawrence and Capt. William Parker for y$^e$ Recrewtinge y$^t$ Regim$^t$ y$^t$ was Leuitna$^{te}$ gen. CROMWELLS, The saddles and pistolls hereafter menconed

By warrant from the Comm$^{ttee}$ for y$^e$ Army dat y$^e$ day and yeere abovesaid ; viz$^t$

| | |
|---|---|
| Saddles pr y$^e$ horse w$^{th}$ their furniture | XXX$^{ty}$ |
| Pistolls compleate w$^{th}$ holsters | XXX$^{ty}$ pr." |

Another of the orders is dated 14th June, the very day of Naseby fight, directing fifty barrels of powder to be sent to the Garrison at Weymouth.

the War; indeed, they might have taken for their motto the words, "A plague on both your houses."

There is no doubt that their sympathies were with the King, but they thought more of the Hearth than of the Throne. As their numbers increased, it occurred to the Royalist gentry and clergy that good party capital could be made of the movement; accordingly "Commissions for raising regiments of Clubmen" were issued, with instructions for extending the project all over the kingdom, and especially into the "Associated Counties." Ultimately the Clubmen increased to 10,000 in number, and means were found by the Royalist party to supply them with arms and to give them some elementary training in their use. Clearly it was high time to pay some attention to this movement, especially as the Clubmen, now openly hostile to Parliament, interposed their forces between Fairfax and Cromwell, thus interfering with their arrangements for stamping out the smouldering remnants of Royalist opposition in the South-west.

On the 3rd July, a deputation of Clubmen waited upon Fairfax at Dorchester, headed by one of their leaders; they affirmed that "it was fit they should show their grievances *and their strength*," and they requested the General to furnish them with safe conducts enabling them to go to the King and to the Parliament. Fairfax felt that they were too strong to be treated cavalierly; he was civil to them, but postponed his reply till the following day, when he refused their request.

It remained for Oliver to give the finishing touch to the Clubmen's organisation. Setting out with a party of horse to meet the Clubmen, he observed colours flying from the top of a difficult hill, and sending an officer with a few men to demand an explanation, and to inform the Clubmen that the Lieutenant-General was present, one of the leaders came down, and said they wanted to know why some of their friends had been taken at Shaftesbury ? To which Oliver replied, "That he held himself not bound to give him or them an account ; what was done was by authority ; and they that did it were not responsible to them that had none ; but not to leave them wholly unsatisfied, he told him, those persons so met had been the occasion and stirrers of many tumultuous and unlawful meetings ; for which they were to be tried by law ; which trial ought not by them to be questioned or interrupted." The leader desired to take the answer back to the Clubmen, whereupon Oliver, with a small party, went with him ; and had conference with them to this purpose : " That whereas they pretended to meet there to save their goods, they took a very ill course for that ; to leave their houses was the way to *lose* their goods ; and it was offered them, that justice should be done upon any who offered them violence ; and as for the gentlemen taken at Shaftesbury, it was only to answer some things they were accused of, which they had done contrary to Law and to the peace of the King- dom. Herewith they seeming to be well satisfied, promised to return to their houses, and accordingly did so.

"These being thus quietly sent home, the Lieu- tenant-General advanced further, to a meeting of a greater number, of about 4,000, who betook themselves to Hambledon Hill, near Shrawton. At the bottom of the Hill, ours met a man with a musket, and asked whither he was going ? He said, to the Club Army ; ours asked, What he meant to do ? He asked what they had to do with that ? Being required to lay down his arms he said, He would first lose his life ; but was not so good as his word, for though he cocked and presented his musket, he was prevented, disarmed and wounded."

**Siege of Bristol—exit Rupert.** The Clubmen were dispersed, and the Army proceeded to the siege of Bristol, where Prince Rupert was busily engaged securing his position, but not for long. The city was stormed on the night of the 10th, and Rupert surrendered the next day, to be "heard of in arms no more." One hundred and fifty cannon and other arms, one hundred barrels of powder, and 4,000 men were captured.

In sending his report to Parliament, Cromwell makes a further appeal for liberty of conscience, saying, " *In things of the mind we look for no compulsion, but that of light and reason.* In other things, God hath put the sword in the Parliament's hands ;— for the terror of evil-doers, and the praise of them that do well." But although Oliver was fast putting down Prelacy and Monarchy, he was as yet powerless to take the sting of persecution out of Presbyterianism.

" Prince Rupert rode out of Bristol amid seas of angry human faces, glooming unutterable things upon him ; growling audibly, in spite of his escort, 'Why not hang *him* ?' For indeed the poor Prince had been necessitated to much plunder ; (it was second nature to him) commanding the 'Elixir of the

BUST OF THE PROTECTOR (MARBLE).
In the Author's Collection.

Blackguardism of the Three Kingdoms,' with very insufficient funds for most part ! He begged 1000 muskets from Fairfax on this occasion to assist his escort in protecting him across the country to Oxford; promising, on his honour, to return them after that service. Fairfax lent the muskets; the Prince did honourably return them, what he had of them,—honourably apologising that so many had deserted on the road, of whom neither man nor musket were recoverable at present." *

At the end of September Cromwell invested Winchester, and prepared to storm it, the Governor refusing to surrender : but after a breach had been made he changed his mind, and Oliver took possession of the city, having lost only twelve men in the siege.

His Report to the Speaker was carried by Hugh Peters, his Secretary, who received £50 for bringing the good news.

"It was at the surrender of Winchester that certain of the captive enemies, having complained of being plundered contrary to Articles, Cromwell had the accused parties (six of his own soldiers) tried ; being all found guilty one of them by lot was hanged, and the other five were marched off to Oxford, to be there disposed of as the Governor saw fit. The Oxford Governor politely returned the five prisoners, ' with an acknowledgment of the Lieutenant-General's nobleness."†

---

* Carlyle. *Letters and Speeches*, vol. i. p. 229.   † Ibid.

# CHAPTER VII.

OLIVER'S most notable success in these closing days of the war was the capture of Basing House, near Basingstoke, along with its owner and brave defender, the tough old Marquis of Winchester. The house was a regular fortress, and for four years had stood repeated sieges, laughing to scorn every attempt of the Parliament to take it. The Marquis was a devoted Catholic, having chapels in both houses (he had recently built a new one, leaving the old one still standing), and all the paraphernalia for celebrating mass—thus giving double offence to the Puritans.

**Basing House, 14th Oct., 1645.**

Basing House, and Dennington Castle at Newbury, had been the terror of the roads leading west ever since the war broke out, necessitating military convoys for all who desired to pass, but now " Brave Oliver is here," and final conclusions are tried. The place is summoned to surrender, and the brave but foolish old Marquis gives a taunting refusal ; and so Oliver, adopting his usual tactics, pours a storm of shot upon the weakest part of the defences, a breach is made, his men pour in, and after a terrible fight, from room to room, in which nearly a hundred of the defenders are slain, the place is captured and the old Marquis, still defiant, is compelled to surrender.

In sending his account of the siege to Parliament, Oliver advised that the whole place should be razed to the ground, as it would take a garrison of 800 men to hold it, and this course was adopted. Farmers, and all who had carts, were invited to take freely of all building material to be found, and very soon only a huge mound of *débris* indicated where this noble old mansion had stood.

Hugh Peters, Cromwell's famous Cornish Chaplain, gives a most interesting account of the place and of the siege.

Mr. Peters was one of those who carried the news of the capture to Parliament, and being requested "to make a relation to the House of Commons," spake as follows:

"That he came into Basing House some time after the storm, and took a view first of the works, which were many, the circumvallation being above a mile in compass. The old house had stood (as it is reputed) two or three hundred years, a nest of idolatry; the new house surpassing that in beauty and stateliness, and either of them fit to make an emperor's court. The rooms before the storm (it seems), in both houses, were all completely furnished; provisions for some years, rather than months; 400 quarters of wheat, bacon, divers rooms full, containing hundreds of flitches; cheese proportionable; with oatmeal, beef, pork; beer, divers cellars full, and that very good. A bed in one room, furnished, which cost £1,300. Popish books many, with copes and such 'utensils'! In truth, the house stood in its full pride; and the enemy was persuaded that it would be the last piece of ground

that would be taken by the Parliament, because they
had so often foiled our forces which had formerly
appeared before it. In the several rooms, and about
the house, there were slain 74, and only one woman,
the daughter of Dr. Griffith, who by her railing pro-
voked our soldiers, then in heat, into a farther
passion. There lay dead upon the ground Major
Cuffle—a man of great account amongst them and a
notorious Papist—slain by the hands of Major
Harrison, that godly and gallant gentleman, and
Robinson the Player, who, a little before the storm,
was known to be mocking and scorning the Parliament and our Army. Eight or nine gentlewomen of
rank, running forth together, were entertained by the
common soldiers somewhat coarsely, yet not un-
civilly considering the action in hand. The plunder
of the soldiers continued till Tuesday night; one
soldier had a hundred and twenty pieces in gold for
his share, others plate, others jewels; among the
rest, one got three bags of silver, which (he being not
able to keep his own counsel) grew to be common
pillage amongst the rest, and the fellow had but one
half-crown left for himself at last. The soldiers sold
the wheat to country people, which they held up at
good rates awhile, but afterwards the market fell, and
there were some abatements for haste; after that, they
sold the household stuff, whereof there was good
store, and the country loaded away many carts; and
they continued a great while fetching out all manner
of household stuff, till they had fetched out all the
stools, chairs, and other lumber, all which they
sold to the country people by piecemeal. In all
these great buildings there was not one iron bar left

in all the windows (save only what were on fire)
before night. And the last work of all was the lead,
and by Thursday morning they had hardly left one
gutter about the house. And what the soldiers left
the fire took hold on, which made more than
ordinary haste, leaving nothing but bare walls and
chimneys in less than twenty-four hours, being occasioned by the neglect of the enemy in quenching a
fireball of ours at first.

"We know not how to give a just account of the
number of persons that were within. For we have
not quite three hundred prisoners, and it may be
have found a hundred slain, whose bodies, some
being covered with rubbish, came not at once to our
view.

"Only, riding to the House on Tuesday night, we
heard divers crying in vaults for quarter; but our
men could neither come to them, nor they to us.
Amongst those that he saw slain, one of their officers
lying on the ground, seeming so exceedingly tall, was
measured : and from his great toe to his crown, was
9 feet in length. The Marquis being pressed, by Mr.
Peters arguing with him, broke out and said, 'That
if the King had no more ground in England but
Basing House, he would adventure as he did, and so
maintain it to the uttermost,'—meaning with these
Papists ; comforting himself in this disaster, 'That
Basing House was called *Loyalty.*' But he was soon
silenced in the question concerning the King and
Parliament, and could only hope 'that the King
might have a day again.' And thus the Lord was
pleased in a few hours to show us what mortal seed
all earthly glory grows upon, and how just and

righteous the ways of God are, who takes sinners in their own snares, and lifteth up the hands of His despised people. This is now the twentieth garrison that hath been taken in this summer by this Army. . . . Mr. Peters presented the Marquis's own colours which he brought from Basing, the motto of which was '*Donec pax redeat terris,*' the very same as King Charles gave upon his Coronation money when he came to the Crown. The House voted Mr. Peters £200 a year for life." *

One of the prisoners taken at Basing was old Inigo Jones, the architect. Faithorne, the engraver of the celebrated picture of *Oliver between the Pillars* and of John Milton's portrait, was also taken prisoner here, and Hollar, the engraver. Both of these men were banished on their refusal to take the oath to the Protector.

During the winter (1645) there was some very hard fighting in the West, for although the Royalist commanders—men like the brave and honourable Sir Ralph Hopton—could not but feel that their master's cause was hopeless, they refused to give it up until stern necessity compelled them.

**Surrender of General Hopton, 14th Mar., 1646.** Fairfax and Cromwell, continuing their victorious march, reduced every strong place in Somersetshire and Devon, finally coming up with Hopton in Cornwall and compelling his surrender with 4,000 men, 2,000 arms, and 20 colours.

In the meantime, where was the King? On leaving Leicester, where he had stayed but a few hours, he wandered somewhat aimlessly about,

* Whitelocke.

finally making for the Welsh borders and Ragland Castle. He there, for the last time, got a small force together, and determined to attempt the relief of Chester, for while that city was in the hands of Parliament there was no hope of help arriving from Ireland. But the battle of Rowton Heath (September, 1645) once again dashed his hopes. Early in the year Montrose, who had had great successes in Scotland, wrote to Charles: "Before the end of the summer I shall be in a position to come to your Majesty's aid with a brave army."

But Montrose had met his match in David Lesley, who utterly routed him near Selkirk, and the poor King was compelled to return to Wales, going from thence to Oxford, which place was still strongly held by Rupert. Fairfax was now ordered to Oxford, reaching there with a powerful force early in May. All the strength of the Royalists was now concentrated in that city, but, immensely strong as it was, its defenders were conscious that the end had arrived, and that their best hope lay in negotiation rather than in fighting.

The King had left the city in disguise at midnight on the 27th April, his wanderings ending for a while in the midst of the Scots army at Newark. On the 20th June the Treaty was signed, and two days after "Rupert and his brother Maurice took the road, with their attendants and their passes to the sea-coast—a sight for the curious.

"The next day 'there went about 300 persons, mostly of quality,' and on the following day all the Royalist force, some to the East and some to the North, with 'drums beating, colours flying' for the last time ; all with passes, with agitated thoughts and outlooks; and in sacred Oxford the 'abomination of desolation' supervened ! Oxford surrendering with the King's sanction quickened other surrenders ; Ragland Castle itself, and the obstinate old Marquis, gave in before the end of August ; and the first Civil War, to the last ember of it, was extinct."*

Parliament being now supreme and the sole authority, proceeded to fill up the vacancies in its ranks caused by the desertion of the Royalist members three years before ; and before the winter about 230 new members had taken their places in the House. Amongst the Royalists these new members were dubbed " Recruiters," in the number being Colonel (afterwards Admiral) Blake, Ireton (married during the recent siege of Oxford to Bridget, Oliver's daughter), Edmund Ludlow, and Algernon Sidney.

* Carlyle.

## CHAPTER VIII.

THE Government of England by Personal rule, both in Church and State, died hard, but it finally ended with the battle of Naseby. Until then, the majority *The Presby-* of the leaders in Parliament, and in- *terian Church* deed of Englishmen generally, would *of England.* have been content with a very moderate limitation of the Royal powers, but the extraordinary ineptitude and wrong-headedness of Charles—his utter want of statesmanship—his unshaken belief in his "star," and reliance on "the divinity that doth hedge a king," made all hope of accommodation with him impossible. Not that he refused to discuss terms; he even agreed to many points demanded of him, but always with the fixed determination to cancel his most solemn engagements when he "became a king again." And yet there are people to this day who prate of Oliver's insincerity, and in the same breath glorify that "most religious Monarch and Martyr" Charles I !

The Scots were rejoiced to have the King in their camp, and their commander immediately left Newark, and marched to Newcastle, where they expected to have him more under their influence; but little did they know the kind of man they had to deal with ! They entreated Charles "with tears," and "on their knees" to take the Covenant, and to sanction the

Presbyterian religion, promising that if he would consent they would fight to the death for him.

The English Parliament—Lords and Commons—who had already taken the Covenant, laid their terms of peace before him, not doubting for a moment of his acceptance. These terms were : " That Parliament should have the command of the Army and Navy for twenty years ; the exclusion of all ' Malignants ' or Royalists who had taken part in the war from Civil and Military office ; the abolition of Episcopacy and the establishment of a Presbyterian Church." *

Not a word about toleration or liberty of conscience, for they intended to give neither. They desired to become the Established Church of England with all its ancient powers and privileges, and while they did not propose to follow Laud in the cropping of Dissenters' ears, they were as determined as he was to suppress them by rigorous fines, imprisonments, and civil disabilities.

But Charles resolutely refused compliance, although his friends and his Queen urged him to accept the conditions. He relied upon the dissensions of his opponents ; he knew that the Army was intensely discontented with the action of Parliament in enforcing the Covenant, and he would bide his time. Writing to one of his friends, he said, " I am not without hope that I shall be able to draw either the Presbyterians or the Independents to side with me for extirpating one another, so that I shall be really King again." His refusal of the terms offered by the Houses was a crushing defeat for the Presby-

* Green, vol. iii. p. 1185.

OLIVER CROMWELL.
From a Dutch engraving, in the Author's Collection.

terians : " What will become of us," asked one of
them, " now that the King has rejected our proposals ? " " What would have become of us,"
retorted an Independent, " had he accepted them ? "

The term " Independent " had but recently come
into use. " Of the 105 ministers who were present
in the Westminster Assembly, only five were Congre-
gational in sympathy, and these were all returned
refugees from Holland." Baxter, at this time, had
not heard of their existence, and Milton never refers
to them in his earlier pamphlets. They were the
" spiritual descendants " of the " Brownists " of
Elizabeth's time. Under the persecution of that
pious monarch, some of the sect had found refuge in
Holland, from whom came the Pilgrim Fathers. In
the middle of James's reign some of the emigrants
ventured back from Holland, where they had
developed their system of independent congregations,
each forming in itself a complete Church ; but the
" Black Terror " of Laud prevented any great spread
of their opinions.

But after the assembling of the Long Parliament
large numbers of the New England emigrants
returned to England, headed by the redoubtable
Hugh Peters, and with such a leader it would be
impossible for them to remain long in obscurity.

Oliver, who, from having been one of the Parliamentary Commanders had now become the " chief
of men," was, of course, an Independent of Independents, having been nursed in the faith, and brought
up with an ever-increasing belief in its Scrip-
tural truth. He hated intolerance, and never lost
an opportunity of impressing upon an unwilling

Parliament the duty of securing absolute freedom of conscience to every peaceable, law-abiding citizen.

In his letter to the Speaker, announcing the result of the fight at Naseby, already referred to, he said : *" He that ventures his life for the liberty of his Country, I wish he trust God for the liberty of his conscience, and you* [Parliament] *for the liberty he fights for."*

The soldiers, largely recruited from amongst substantial farmers, and mainly Puritans, had taken up arms with very definite ideas as to what they wanted; and they knew that if a Presbyterian Parliament settled with the King, their interests—the interests of the Independents—would be sacrificed. They knew full well that escape from Episcopacy to fall under Presbyterian control, was like getting out of the frying-pan into the fire. They, and the Baptists, were the Dissenters of that day, and Milton voiced their opinions exactly when he wrote that the *"New Presbyter was but old Priest, writ large."*

But amidst all the strife of arms, of tongues, and of Protocols, Oliver was perfectly clear as to his own course, and equally determined to follow it ; and that course was, to be *"*unswervingly true to his great design ; to secure responsible government without anarchy, and freedom of conscience without intolerance.*"*

Any arrangement with the King from whatever party it proceeded, must of necessity be ratified by Parliament, which was still the outward and visible sign of authority.

But since the Self-denying Ordinance was passed, Parliament had become almost exclusively Presbyterian, with decided Monarchical leanings.

And now its leaders thought they saw their opportunity. The Scots Army—of course Presbyterian—was still in England, and had control of the King's **The Scots surrender Charles to Parliament, 1647=48.** person. On their own account the Scots had given up all hope of coming to an agreement with the King, and in face of the fact that the General Assembly absolutely refused to receive one who would not subscribe to the Covenant, the question arose, what is to become of him? for he was daily becoming an increasing source of trouble and embarrassment.

If, therefore, Parliament could disband the Army and obtain possession of the King's person by carrying out the Treaty of December, 1646, in which they undertook to pay the Scots Army £400,000 as the condition of their immediate return to Scotland, the ball would be at their feet.

Accordingly, in January, 1647-48, Major-General Skippon took £200,000, as an instalment, to New-castle, which was accepted by the Scots, who thereupon handed the King over to the Parliament, and returned to their own country.

The Scots having been disposed of, the next thing was to disband the New Model Army, and so relegate its leaders to private life ; to deprive Independency of all corporate action ; and, at the same time, to raise forces in the city to defend it against the Army. The disbandment accomplished, a new Army was to be raised, and under Presbyterian officers was to be sent to Ireland to quell the rebellion there.

But Holles and the other Presbyterian leaders

in the House had reckoned without their host, for the Army declined disbandment until their just claims had been attended to. They had been without pay for a year, and had maintained themselves to a large extent from their own resources. They were not by any means ordinary soldiers, having come from their farms and other occupations at a direct call from God, as they honestly believed, and they did not intend to separate until their work was done.

It was to obtain liberty of conscience and freedom from kingly tyranny that they had taken up arms, in which cause "so many of their friends' lives had been lost, and so much of their own blood had been spilt," and they declined to disband until these objects had been secured, and if need be they would again act together to secure them. A deputation from the Army pleaded passionately at the Bar of the House, that, "On becoming soldiers we have not ceased to be citizens."

The Council of Officers urged Parliament to listen to the men's proposals, but all in vain; so the Army took the matter into their own hands. Setting aside the Council of Officers, and appointing in its place a Council of "Agitators, or Agents," each regiment sending two members, a general meeting of the Army was summoned at Triploe Heath, and the proposals made by the Parliament were rejected with cries of "Justice."

While this was going on, a rumour reached the Army that the King was to be removed to London, a new Army raised, and a new Civil War begun.

This roused them to madness. Five hundred troopers suddenly appeared before Holmby House, where the King was residing in charge of the Parliamentary Commissioners, and displaced its guards.

"Where is your commission for this act?" Charles asked the Cornet who commanded them.

*"It is behind me,"* said Joyce, pointing to his soldiers.

*"It is written in very fine and legible characters,"* laughed the King. The seizure had, in fact, been previously concerted between Charles and the "Agitators."

"I will part willingly," he told Joyce, "if the soldiers confirm all that you have promised me. You will exact from me nothing that offends my conscience or my honour."

"It is not our maxim," replied the Cornet, "to constrain the conscience of anyone, still less that of our King."

The Parliament was terror-stricken, and Cromwell, who had relinquished his command and retired from the Army before the close of the war, was hotly accused of having caused the mutiny, and it was even proposed to arrest him. He defended himself with vehemence, but feeling he was in the midst of enemies, prudently betook himself to the Army, and on the 25th June was in full march on London.

The demands of the Army were clearly set forth in a "humble representation" addressed to the Houses:

"We desire a settlement of the Peace of the Kingdom and of the liberties of the subject, according to

the votes and declarations of Parliament.    We desire
no alteration in the Civil Government; as little do we
desire to interrupt or in the least to intermeddle with
the settling of the Presbyterial Government."

At this juncture, Ireton, Cromwell's son-in-law,
took up the thread of negotiations with Charles.
He was a very able man, both with pen and
sword ; a B.A. of Trinity College, Oxford, and a
student of the Middle Temple.    As a Member of
Parliament, he had a peculiarly statesmanlike grasp
of public questions; a man of great and studied
moderation, and one who well knew how far to go
in the hour of victory.    It would have been well
for Charles if he had suffered himself to be
guided by Ireton; for, indeed, it was his only
chance.

Remarking to the King that *"there must be some
difference between conquerors and conquered,"* he proceeded to lay before him his views of what the
situation demanded.    Seven "delinquents" were to
be banished, and all the rest to be covered by an Act
of Oblivion—a strange contrast to the action of the
Royalists after the *Blessed* Restoration—Parliament to
have control of the Army and Navy for ten years and
to nominate the great officers of State ; full liberty
of conscience to be secured to all, and the Acts compelling attendance at Church, the taking of the
Covenant, and the compulsory use of the Prayer
Book, to be repealed ; triennial Parliaments, a fair
re-distribution of seats, and the re-adjustment of
taxation, with simplification of judicial procedure—
these were the main points of Ireton's proposals,
and Cromwell heartily supported him.

The King would have none of it ; with inconceivable fatuity he said to Ireton, " *You cannot do without me— you are lost if I do not support you.*" His self-confidence was speedily explained : a sudden incursion of London rabble was made upon Parliament, which was forced to recall the eleven members recently ejected. A number of Peers and a hundred Commoners fled to the Army, while the remaining members prepared to repel it and invited Charles to London.

But clever as the ruse was, the conspirators were not sufficiently clever to overcome the difference between an Army *in esse* and one *in posse,* and the news had no sooner reached the camp than the march on London was begun. "*In two days,*" said Oliver, "*the city will be in our hands.*"

Arriving at Hounslow, the Army was met by the Speakers of both Houses of Parliament, who were received with shouts of approval.

In the City great excitement prevailed, the ardour of the Royalist party having been greatly damped by the refusal of Southwark to join them, on the plea of being outside the City.

Massey, the commander of the City troops, sent out scouts to report upon the movements of the Army, and when word was brought that they had halted, the people cried "*One and All*"—stick together—but when the march was resumed, they cried even more lustily, "*Treat, treat, treat !*" "So they spent most part of the night. At last they resolved to send the General an humble Letter, beseeching him that there might be a way of composure."*

* Whitelocke.

Next day (17th Sept., 1647-48), the Civic authorities and Parliamentary "*remainders,*" made submission at Holland House, Kensington, after which the Army marched three deep by Hyde Park, into the heart of the City, "with boughs of laurel in their hats"; and all was ended. The headquarters of the Army are changed to Putney; one of its outer posts is Hampton Court, where his Majesty, obstinate still, but somewhat despondent now of getting the two Parties to extirpate one another, is lodged.*

"Saturday, Sept. 18th. After a sermon in Putney Church, the General, many great officers, field officers, inferior officers and adjutators, met in the Church, debated the Proposals of the Army towards a settlement of this *bleeding nation*; altered some things in them, and were very full of the Sermon, which had been preached by Mr. Peters." †

Notwithstanding the recent events in the City and at Westminster, in which Charles's complicity was strongly suspected, Cromwell continued his visits to Hampton Court. He was sincerely desirous of an accommodation by which Monarchy might be re-established under constitutional guarantees, for he saw clearly the difficulties that would ensue upon its abolition.

But the Army, composed of soldiers and not statesmen, could only see in Charles the chief cause of their having been taken from their farms and merchandise, and of the blood that had been shed, and they began to be suspicious of, and to resent Cromwell's visits; he therefore discontinued them, although he had not lost all faith in Charles.

* Carlyle.          † Whitelocke.

But now, events were about to occur which fully justified the Army's suspicions of the King and entirely destroyed Oliver's faith in his sincerity.

Rumours came from Scotland that an army was ready to march into England in the King's interest, and projected risings in various parts of the country began to assume definite shape, when suddenly, the whole nation was startled by the announcement that the King had escaped.

## CHAPTER IX.

A MUTINOUS spirit had already shown itself in the Army, a large body amongst the soldiers—

*Flight of the King, 11th Nov., 1647.* the Levellers—loudly demanding the punishment of the King as the "*Chief Delinquent*"; but they now became excited to frenzy, and broke out into actual mutiny at Ware. Cromwell and other chief officers appeared on the scene, fully recognising the danger, and at once ordered eleven of the mutineers to stand out of the ranks; they were tried by Court-martial on the field; "three of them condemned to be shot—throw dice for their life, and one is shot, there and then."

Even Oliver was now convinced of Charles's incurable duplicity, and exclaimed, "The King is a man of great parts, and great understanding, but so great a dissembler, and so false a man, that he is not to be trusted."

Poor Strafford, as he laid his neck on the block at Tower Hill, exclaimed in bitterness of spirit, "*Put not your trust in Princes*"; and now Oliver has come to the same conclusion, after having done his utmost, at great peril to himself, to save the King from the consequences of his own obstinate folly.

On leaving Hampton Court at nine o'clock, the King rode on for the whole night and the next day, not knowing where to go—a pitiable spectacle, truly !—but—having some knowledge of Colonel Robert Hammond, the Governor of the Isle of Wight,—he decided to deliver himself up to him. Hammond reported the event to Parliament, and was ordered to confine the King in Carisbrooke Castle.

On the 3rd January, 1647-48, the House of Commons voted, *1st.* That they will make no more addresses to the King ; *2nd.* None shall apply to him without leave of the two Houses, upon pain of being guilty of High Treason ; *3rd.* They will receive nothing from the King, nor shall any other bring anything to them from him, nor receive anything from the King.

War, and rumours of war, abounded, and even reached the Royal prisoner in Carisbrooke, causing him to be restless, and, not unnaturally, anxious to be abroad again. On the 20th March, aided by some of his attendants, he tried to get through the bars of the window of his apartment, " but his breast was so big the bar would not give him passage," and so the attempt failed.

**Secono Civil War, April, 1648.** It had become evident that the war would have to be fought over again, and under circumstances of exceeding peril for Cromwell and his friends. " Elements of destruction everywhere, under and around them ; their lot either to conquer or ignominiously to die. A King not to be bargained with ; kept in Carisbrooke, the centre of all factious hopes, of world-wide intrigues ; that is one element. A great Royalist Party, subdued with difficulty, and ready at all

moments to rise again, that is another. A great
Presbyterian Party, at the head of which is London
City, '*the Purse-bearer of the Cause*,' highly dissatisfied at the course things had taken, and looking
desperately around for new combinations, and a new
struggle ; reckon that for a third element. Add
lastly a headlong Mutineer, Republican, or Levelling
Party ; and consider that there is a working House
of Commons which counts about seventy, divided
into pretty equal halves too." *

The peril was so obvious, and so serious, that it had
the immediate effect of welding the Army together
again, and at a great meeting of the Army Leaders
held at Windsor on the eve of their march against
the revolt, they came to the resolution, " That it was
our duty, if ever the Lord brought us back again in
peace, to call Charles Stuart, that man of blood, to
account for the blood he has shed, and mischief he
has done to his utmost against the Lord's cause and
people in these poor nations."

The King had signed a secret treaty with the Scots,
making them large promises which he never intended
to keep, and Duke Hamilton set out with an Army
of 20,000 men to invade England. Immediately
there were risings in Wales, Kent, Essex, and
other places; London was in a state of siege, and
confusion reigned everywhere. Hamilton took
Carlisle and Berwick, and the Royal cause had never
looked more promising. But in a few days Fairfax
had crushed the Kentish rebels, and driven those in
the Eastern county inside the strong walls of
Colchester.

* Carlyle.

SIEGE OF PONTEFRACT CASTLE.

HOLOGRAPH LETTER OF OLIVER CROMWELL.

**Battle of Preston, Aug., 1648.** Cromwell, having crushed the revolt in Wales, proceeded northwards to meet Duke Hamilton and his 20,000 Scots, and joining Lambert in Yorkshire, he gave battle at Preston.

For three days the fight continued, extending over thirty miles of country, the Scots army advancing in a long straggling line, being unaware of Oliver's presence until he had cut it in two—rolling one half back north and the other toward the south.

Cromwell's army was vastly inferior in numbers, was weary and footsore after its forced march from Wales, but "brave Oliver" was there, and thanks to his splendid tactics and superior genius, and to the divided councils in the Scots army, he out-generalled Hamilton, utterly destroying his army— now increased to 24,000 men—and captured the Duke and most of his officers. The Duke being also Earl of Cambridge, was tried for treason in levying war against his country, and executed.

After a rapid march to Edinburgh, Oliver came south again,—taking Berwick and Carlisle *en route*, but failing to take Pontefract Castle, not having a siege train,—and being urgently wanted in London, where the supreme crisis of the long struggle was at last imminent.

**Siege of Pontefract Castle, 1645.** The first siege of Pontefract Castle, which lasted five months, and proved one of the most difficult operations of the war, terminated in its surrender in July, 1645, when the garrison was permitted to march away to Newark. Everything was left in the Castle except such property belonging to the officers as "did not exceed what a cloak bag will contain."

Sir Thomas Fairfax was appointed Governor, and he installed Colonel Cotterall as his deputy; all went well until the summer of 1648, when—aided by the treachery of John Morris, late an officer in the Parliamentary Army,—the Castle was surprised and retaken on behalf of the King. Morris was now appointed Governor, and he lost no time in strengthening the defences, and laying in store of provisions, well knowing that he would not long remain undisturbed. The command of the forces operating against the Castle devolved upon General Lambert, until he was called away to Scotland in consequence of the Hamilton outbreak; then Sir Henry Cholmley and Colonel Charles Fairfax, a relative of the Lord General's, had joint command, but were not altogether harmonious in their actions. In November, Cromwell spent some time in the neighbourhood, but found that the Parliamentary Army was neither sufficiently supplied with guns and ammunition, nor strong enough to attempt the storming of the fortress; he therefore induced Parliament to send further supplies of men and munitions. I have in my possession a collection of MSS.—nearly two hundred in number—dealing with the siege of Pontefract Castle; among them are several letters written by Cromwell while there, two of which bear eloquent witness to his kindness of heart when appealed to on behalf of the sick and suffering. The letters speak for themselves :—

"Sr, The bearer, Mrs. Gray is desirous to goe into ye Castle to see a brother of hers who lyes sick in the Castle. I desire you would let her have a

SIEGE OF PONTEFRACT CASTLE.

HOLOGRAPH LETTER OF OLIVER CROMWELL.

In the Author's Collection.

Drumme and give her your pass to returne within a limited time. I rest, Sr, Yr very humble servt.

"O. Cromwell.

" Knottingly, Nov : ye 11th, 1648."

In the next case a poor woman begs for relief from the excessive assessment for the support of the soldiery :

" The bearer has been with me complaining exceedingly of her poverty as not able to get victuals for her familye and yet is forced to maintain sold : much beyond her ability. I desire that what favor can be afforded her you would doe it.

"At the desire of yr humble servt ·

" O. Cromwell.

" ffor the honoble. Col : Charles Ffairfax

" at Pontefract. these."

There are many other interesting letters in this collection, some of which throw a curious light upon the relations existing between the opposing Commanders. Sir John Digby, one of the Royalist officers in the Castle, writes to Colonel Charles Fairfax, commanding the besiegers :—

" Sr, You sent us shells before you sent me egges, my hearty thankes to you for them ; and ye rather yor shells haveinge not done us soe much harme, as one of yor egges will doe mee good, blessed be god ; Sr, I have sent you money for them, and ye allmanacke by this Drumme, and shall crave yor pardon if when these fourteene egges are spent, I send for ye rest of ye shilling's worth promised, hopeing they will prove to bee three a penny at ye least."

Having made arrangements for a closer siege of the Castle, and reinstating Lambert in command,

Oliver hastened to London, where his presence was now urgently required in connection with the trial of Charles.

No sooner had the news of the death of the King reached the garrison at Pontefract than they proclaimed Charles II. and struck silver coins in honour of the event. These coins, which are extremely rare, are noteworthy as being the first that bore the name of Charles II. *

In March, Lambert summoned the garrison to surrender, offering them favourable terms, but excluding six of their number—including Governor Morris. Lambert was asked to give the excepted officers six days in which to endeavour to escape, and good-naturedly consented. In the result, Morris and another succeeded, one was killed and the three others hid themselves until after the surrender (25th March, 1649), and then escaped. On being recaptured, Morris was tried at York on a charge of High Treason, and hanged.

Parliament voted Lambert £300 a year for life, and ordered the famous old Castle to be demolished.

Frederic Harrison (from whose admirable work on the Protector I have frequently quoted) well says :

"To Cromwell the second Civil War was the unpardonable sin. God had manifested His will in the triumph of the Army. To be slack, to be indulgent, was to struggle against His will, to struggle against the manifestation was to tempt God. The Ironsides were returning home to keep their word ; and

---

° One of them—a shilling—is in the Author's collection.

Cromwell was now as deeply resolved as any man to exact the uttermost farthing."

But victories against the Royal cause were accepted in a half-hearted way by Parliament, which had become increasingly Presbyterian, and more than ever alarmed at the growing power of the Army, composed, as it was, mainly of Independents, friends of Religious Liberty. While Cromwell was away fighting, Parliament passed the most atrocious Acts against all forms of Dissent—Acts that Laud himself would have stood aghast at. It decreed *Death* for all who denied the doctrine of the Trinity, or of the Divinity of Christ, or the resurrection of the body, or of a Day of Judgment ! At the very moment of the great victory at Preston, the House of Lords was engaged in discussing charges of treason against Cromwell, while Commissioners were again sent to the Isle of Wight to conclude peace with the King.

" Royalists and Presbyterians alike pressed Charles to grasp the easy terms which were now offered him. But his hopes from Scotland had only broken down to give place to hopes of a new war with the aid of an army from Ireland, and the negotiators saw forty days wasted in useless chicanery. ' *Nothing,*' Charles wrote to his friends, ' *is changed in my designs.*'"

But with the surrender of Colchester, and Cromwell's convention with Argyle, the war was over, and as the soldiers unbuckled their armour, they vowed that the " *Chief Delinquent*" should be brought to justice. "Now or never" became the watchword of the Army ; their pay was nine months in arrear, they were about to be disbanded, and all their struggles and privations rendered nugatory.

On the 16th October, the soldiers drew up and presented to Fairfax, "The Articles and charge of the Officers and Soldiers of the Armie concerning the King's Majestie and all persons whatsoever, who shall endeavour to re-inthrone him," until he shall have been cleared from the charge of shedding innocent blood.

**The Army's Articles against the King, Oct., 1648.**

The General was also requested to insist upon payment of what was due to the Army, and to abolish its free quartering upon the people. This letter was duly read in the Commons and the last part only taken cognisance of, for it was resolved, that the soldiery be forthwith satisfied, speedy care to be taken for settling their arrears.

Soon the Army was at Windsor, on its way to London, after having sent to Parliament a strong *Remonstrance* against its treaty with the King.

Then Charles, after vain attempts to escape from Carisbrooke, was confined, a close prisoner, in Hurst Castle. The House rejects the Remonstrance and presently finds the Army encamped at Whitehall; the treaty with the King is approved after an all-night sitting, and then Palace Yard is occupied by a regiment of horse, and Colonel Pride, with his regiment of foot, is quartered in Westminster Hall.

**Pride's Purge, Dec. 6th, 1648.**

Says Carlyle: "Wednesday 6th December, 1648. Col. Rich's regiment of horse, and Colonel Pride's regiment of foot, were a guard to the Parliament; and the City trainbands were discharged from that employment. Yes, they were! Colonel Rich's horse stand ranked in the Palace Yard, Colonel Pride's foot in

Westminster Hall, and at all entrances to the
Commons House, this day ; and in Colonel Pride's
hand is a written list of names—names of the chief
among the hundred and twenty-nine ; and at his side
is my Lord Grey of Groby, who, as this Member
after that comes up, whispers, or beckons, '*He is one
of them, he cannot enter !*' And Pride gives the word,
'*To the Queen's Court,*' and member after member is
marched thither, forty-one of them, this day ; and
kept there in a state bordering on *rabidity*, asking, By
what Law ? and ever again, By what Law ? . . .
Hugh Peters visits them ; has little comfort, no Light
as to the Law ; confesses, 'It is by the Law of
Necessity ' ; truly, by the Power of the Sword."

"Pride's Purge" had cleared the House of the
King's party, and henceforth the Army is master.

The breaking out of the Second Civil War, through
the direct agency of Charles, finally drove Oliver into
the ranks of his most determined opponents, and the
trial and punishment of the "Chief Delinquent"
became inevitable.

# CHAPTER X.

Trial of the King, Jan. 20, 1648=49. THE final scenes in the great drama open on the 20th January, 1648-9, by the constitution of the High Court of Justice in Westminster Hall, Serjeant John Bradshaw being the President.

"The Act of the Commons in Parliament for the trial of the King, was read after the Court was called, each member rising up as he was named. The King came into the Court with his hat on, the Serjeant ushering him with the Mace ; Colonel Hacker and about thirty officers and gentlemen more came as his guard." The President, addressing the King, informed him that he was to hear the charge made against him, when the Court would proceed. The Solicitor-General then read the charge, amid some interruption on the King's part, and on hearing himself described as Traitor, Tyrant, Murderer, and Public Enemy, he smiled contemptuously. After a long wrangle between the President and the King, who objected to the competency of the Court to try him, an adjournment was ordered over the Sunday. Considerable sensation was caused, during the reading of the

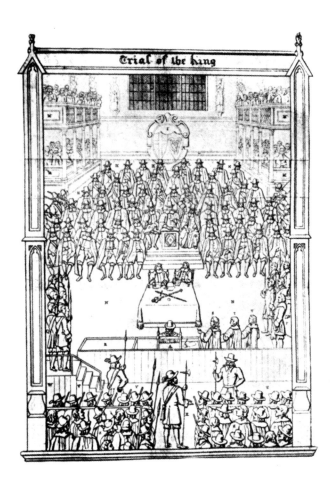

WESTMINSTER HALL,

20 JAN. 1628-9.

Charge, by the falling off of the head of the King's staff, which, no one offering to take up, he stooped for it himself, none so low as to do him reverence. As he walked down the Hall, some cried, "God save the King"; but many more cried, "*Justice.*" On the Monday the Court resumed, and on the King entering the Hall, a great shout was raised, the Captain of the Guard being charged to maintain silence. The wrangle was continued, and the King still "required" to know the authority under which the Court acted.

*The President:* "Sir, 'tis not for prisoners to 'require.'"

*The King:* "Prisoners! Sir, I am not an ordinary prisoner."

And as the King would not plead, the officer was ordered to remove his prisoner.

On the third day the King came in with his guard, "looking with an austere countenance upon the Court, and sits down," and the same wrangle continued, the King refusing to plead, or to acknowledge the authority of the Court. Once again it was adjourned, the Public Cryer saying, "God bless the *Kingdom* of England."

On the fourth day, on the opening of the Court, the President appeared in a scarlet vesture "befitting the business of the day." As the King passed up the Hall, a cry was made for "Justice and Execution."

The President, having recapitulated the proceedings of the previous days, and having stated that the King was there on a charge of Treason and other crimes against the people of England, a malignant lady* interrupted the Court, saying, "*Not half the people,*"

* Generally believed to have been Lady Fairfax.

but was soon silenced, and then, having stated that the Court had come to a conclusion as to their course, the President asked if the prisoner had anything to say why sentence should not be passed upon him.

The King then said he had somewhat to communicate to the Lords and Commons, which might lead to the peace of the Kingdom, and asked for an adjournment.

This was accordingly granted, and half-an-hour afterwards the Court resumed, when the President stated his intention to proceed to the sentence without further delay. He then explained the grounds upon which the capital sentence was founded, and ordered the Clerk to read it to the prisoner :

"That whereas the Commons of England in Parliament had appointed them an High Court of Justice for the trying of Charles Stuart, King of England, before whom he had been three times convented, and at the first time a charge of High Treason and other crimes and misdemeanours was read in the behalf of the Kingdom of England ; for all which Treasons and Crimes this Court doth adjudge, that he, the said Charles Stuart, as a Tyrant, Traitor, Murtherer, and a Public Enemy, shall be put to death by the severing of his head from his body."

The King again tried to speak, but was not permitted, and was taken to his lodgings.

Outside Whitehall, 30th Jan., 1648=49.    And now comes the last sad scene. On Tuesday, the 30th January, 1648, about ten in the morning, the King was brought from St. James's, walking through the

Park, with a regiment of foot, part before and part behind him, with colours flying, drums beating, his private guard with some of his gentlemen before and some behind, bareheaded, Dr. Juxon next behind him, and Colonel Thomlinson (who had charge of him) talking with the King, bareheaded.

Then going up the stairs into the Gallery, and so into the Cabinet Chamber where he used to lie, he went to his devotions, refusing to dine (having before taken the Sacrament) ; about an hour before he came forth he drank a glass of claret and ate a piece of bread. From thence he was accompanied by Dr. Juxon through the Banqueting House to the scaffold, which was covered with black velvet. The axe and block had been set in the middle of the scaffold. The ground was kept by foot and horse soldiers, and the multitude of spectators was very great. The King being come upon the scaffold, looked very earnestly on the block and asked " *if there were no higher block ?* " He then delivered a speech in which he asserted his innocence of the crimes laid to his charge.

Turning to Colonel Hacker, the King said, " *Take care that they do not put me to pain.*" Just then a gentleman coming near the axe, the King said, " *Take heed of the axe, pray take heed of the axe.*" Then the King, turning to Dr. Juxon, said, " I have a good cause, and a gracious God on my side."

*Dr. J.* There is but one stage more. This stage is turbulent and troublesome ; it is a short one, but you may consider it will soon carry you a very great way ; it will carry you from earth to heaven, and there you shall find a great deal of cordial joy and comfort.

*The King.* I go from a corruptible to an incorruptible crown, where no disturbance can be; no disturbance in the world.

*Dr. J.* You are exchanged from a temporal to an eternal crown—a good exchange.

The King then said to the executioner, "Is my hair well?" Then he took off his cloak and his George,* giving the latter to Dr. Juxon, saying, "Remember."

Then the King put off his doublet, and being in his waistcoat, put his cloak on again; then looking upon the block, said to the executioner, "You must set it fast."

*Executioner.* It *is* fast, sir.

*King.* It might have been a little higher.

*Executioner.* It *can* be no higher, sir.

*King.* When I put out my hands, this way—(stretching them out) then—

After that, having said two or three words to himself with hands and eyes lift up, immediately stooping down, laid his neck upon the block; and then the executioner again putting his hair under his cap, the King said, "Stay for the sign."

*Executioner.* Yes, I will, and it please your Majesty.

And after a very little pause the King stretched forth his hands—the executioner, at one blow, severed his head from the body.

After the King's head was cut off, the executioner held it up and showed it to the spectators, when the body was put into a coffin covered with black velvet.

* This coin or medal was sold at Sotheby's in November, 1896, and realised more than £700.

EXECUTION OF THE KING.
From a rare print.

In speaking of the King's execution and of Cromwell's share in the proceedings, Frederic Harrison remarks :

" To him and to his Ironsides to bring the King to judgment was no mere act of earthly justice. . . . For seven years the land had swam in blood, ruin and confusion. And of all that, Charles Stuart was the root and contriver. But Cromwell was not only a Puritan, saturated with Biblical canons of morality and justice, he was also a profound statesman.

" He had struggled, against hope and inclination, for a monarchic settlement of the grand dispute. Slowly he had come to know, not only that the man, Charles Stuart, was incurably treacherous, but that any settlement of Parliament with the old Feudal Monarchy was impossible. As the head of the King rolled on the scaffold the old Feudal Monarchy expired for ever. In January, 1648-49, a great mark was set in the course of the National life—the Old Rule behind it, the New Rule before it. Parliamentary Government, the consent of the nation, equality of rights, and equity in the law, all date from this great New Departure. The Stuarts indeed returned for one generation, but with the sting of the old monarchy gone, and only to disappear, almost without a blow.

" The Church of England returned, but not the Church of Laud or of Charles.

" The Peers returned, but as a meek House of Lords, with their castles razed, their feudal rights and their political power extinct. It is said that the Regicides killed Charles I. only to make Charles II.

king. It is not so. They killed the Old Monarchy ; and the restored monarch was by no means its heir, but a royal Stadtholder, or hereditary President. In 1648-49, when Charles I. ceased to live, the true monarchy of England ceased to reign. Oliver Cromwell was for ten years supreme ruler ; whilst Charles II. was a despised and forgotten exile. The monarchies, peerages, and churches of the civilised world, roared with horror and rage ; but in five years the rage was spent, and England was settling into new lines, which might possibly have been permanent, and which certainly prepared her present constitutional system. The solemn judgment of Charles Stuart as a traitor to his people, as a public officer who had criminally abused his trust, gave a new life to the history of England, and ultimately to the modern history of Europe."

And Carlyle :

" Thus ends the second Civil War. In Regicide, in a Commonwealth, and Keepers of the Liberties of England. In punishment of delinquents, in abolition of cobwebs ;—if it be possible, in a government of heroism and veracity ; at lowest, of anti-flunkeyism, anti-cant, and the endeavour after heroism and veracity."

Who performed the office of executioner on Charles I.? The question has been often asked, but has never been absolutely answered.

The principal persons engaged in his trial and execution are, of course, well known, but who was the headsman ?

Very few historical secrets have been so well kept, and there is no doubt that the fact of its having been kept points to the existence of a wide divergence of public opinion on the policy, or lawfulness, of taking the life of the sovereign.

Of course it was no new thing for crowned heads to be consigned to the headsman's axe, but hitherto it had been done only by other crowned heads.

Henry VIII. had cut off the heads of numerous queens, and Queen Bess herself had effectually destroyed the myth of "the divinity that doth hedge a king," by taking the life of Charles's own grandmother, Mary, Queen of Scots. But then, of course,

> " That in the captain 's but a choleric word,
> Which in the soldier is flat blasphemy,"

and was it not the height of audacity that the Sovereign People should follow the example, so recently set, of the Sovereign Individual?*

Anyhow, the deed was done, and the question is, Who did it?

---

* Charles himself was not above taking advantage of that most atrocious of crimes, the judicial murder of Sir Walter Raleigh, one of the noblest of that band of Englishmen who made the reign of Elizabeth illustrious. In order to promote his suit with the Spanish Infanta, Charles was base enough to permit the sacrifice of the old hero to the malignant hate of that foe of his and of England who could never face Raleigh in the field.

Carlyle, describing the murder—which took place in the Old Palace Yard on the 29th October, 1618—says : " A very tragic scene. Such a man, with his head grown grey, with his strong heart breaking, still strength enough in it to break with dignity. Somewhat proudly he laid his old grey head on the block, as if saying in better than words ' There, then!' The Sheriff offered to let him warm himself again within doors at a fire (the morning was cold and frosty). ' Nay, let us be swift,' said Raleigh; ' in few minutes my ague will return upon me, and if I be not dead before that, they will say I tremble for fear.' "—*Letters and Speeches*, vol. i. p. 46.

Though Joyce and Hugh Peters have been, absurdly enough, suspected of inflicting the fatal blow on Charles, and though another claimant **Richard** for this distinction is put for- **Brandon.** ward in the *Gentleman's Magazine* for 1767, there seems little doubt that Richard Brandon, the common hangman, assisted by his man, Ralph Jones, a ragman in Rosemary Lane, in fact, perpetrated the deed. Among the tracts, relative to the Civil War, presented to the British Museum by George III. in 1762, are three on this subject, which are fully noticed in a note to Mr. Ellis's *Letters on English History*, vol. iii. (second series). It appears by the register of Whitechapel Church, that Richard Brandon was buried there on the 24th of June, 1649 ; and a marginal note (not in the hand of the Registrar, but bearing the mark of antiquity) states: "This R. Brandon is supposed to have cut off the head of Charles I." One of the tracts, entitled, "The Confessions of Richard Brandon, the Hangman, upon his Death-bed, concerning the Beheading of his late Majesty," printed in 1649, states: "During the time of his sickness, his conscience was much troubled, and exceedingly perplexed in mind : and on Sunday last a young man of his acquaintance, going to visit him, fell into discourse, asked him how he did and whether he was not troubled in conscience for having cut off the King's head. He replied, yes, by reason that (upon the time of his tryall) he had taken a vow and protestation, wishing God to punish him, body and soul, if ever he appeared on the scaffold to do the act, or lift up his hand against him. He likewise

confessed that he had £30 for his pains, all paid him
in half-crowns within an hour after the blow was
given ; and he had an orange stuck full with cloves,
and a handkircher out of the King's pocket, so soon
as he was carried off the scaffold ; for which orange
he was proffered 20 shillings by a gentleman in
Whitechapel, but refused the same, and afterwards
sold it for ten shillings in Rosemary Lane. About
eight o'clock that night he returned home to his
wife, living in Rosemary Lane, and gave her the
money, saying it was the dearest money he earned in
his life, for it would cost him his life. About three
days before he died, he lay speechless, uttering many
a sigh and heavy groan, and so in a desperate state
departed from his bed of sorrow. For the burial
whereof great store of wines were sent in by the
Sheriff of the City of London, and a great multitude
of people stood wayting to see his corpse carried to
the churchyard, some crying out, 'Hang him,
rogue,'—'Bury him in the dunghill'; others pressing upon him, saying they would quarter him for
executing the King, insomuch that the church-
wardens and masters of the parish were fain to come
for the suppressing of them ; and with great difficulty
he was at last carried to Whitechapel churchyard,
having (as it is said) a branch of rosemary at each
end of the coffin, on the top thereof, with a rope
crosse from one end to the other. A merry conceited
cook, living at the sign of the Crown, having a black
fan, (worth the value of 30s.) took a resolution to
rent the same in pieces ; and to every feather tied a
piece of packthread, dyed in black ink, and gave
them to divers persons, who, in derision, for a while

wore them in their hats." The second tract states that the first victim Brandon beheaded was the Earl of Strafford.

In the East of London it is clear that the name of Cromwell had less influence than in most of the Courts of Europe.

More difficult than the question as to who was Charles's executioner, is that of the position in which he received the fatal stroke. I have in my possession eight books, some of them published immediately after the execution, and the others a few years subsequently, from which I give extracts :

In the "*Tragicum Theatrum*" (Amsterdam, 1649), the plate shows the King kneeling : "He suddenly knelt down and lay with his neck on the block."

In a pamphlet entitled "*King Charles's Speech made upon the scaffold, 30th January, 1648 :*" "Immediately stooping down he laid his head upon the Block."

*Heath's Chronicle* gives the same words.

In "*Histoire entière et veritable Du Procez de Charles Stuart, Roy d'Angleterre*": "*Il se coucha incontinent après sur le ventre.*"

Another French account says, "*Mettoit son col sur le tronc.*"

In a book published in Utrecht in 1692, these words occur: "*Après cela il se mit à genoux sur le marchpié du billot.*" And in this account it is added that the block was provided with four iron rings, for the purpose of tying the King by the hands and feet in case he should offer resistance.

In Sanderson's "*Compleat History of the Life and Raigne of King Charles from his cradle to his grave,*" published in 1658, it is stated that Charles "stooped down to the block as to a Prayer desk."

From a book published in Paris in 1650, I extract the following :—"*Levant les mains, et les yeux, il se pancha et mit son col sur le billot.*" *

---

* One of the most interesting accounts of the events lead-ing up to the trial and execution of the King, and of the execution itself is to be found in the January number of the *Cornhill Magazine*, 1897, by C. H. Firth.

# CHAPTER XI.

In dealing with a period of history more or less remote, there is a natural tendency to judge of the actions of men by the standard of our own time. The early history of the Quakers is a case in point. The action of many of the leading members of the new sect, in holding public discussions with ministers of the dominant churches, in presence of their congregations, would now be rightly considered an indecent and disorderly proceeding, but in the days of the Commonwealth it was a very common occurrence, and by no means confined to the Quakers. Again, in considering the attitude of Cromwell towards the Roman Catholics, both in England and Ireland, it is necessary to take into consideration the religious history of his time and of the generation preceding it. Coming of a strong Puritan family, Oliver was born only eleven years after the defeat of the Armada, when the memory of the "Spanish fury" under Philip and Mary was still fresh in the minds of men. Gunpowder Plot had yet to be hatched, and although James escaped the fate designed for him, his matrimonial coquettings with Catholic Powers on behalf of Charles, his readiness to shed the best Protestant

From the original drawing by Cooper, in the possession of
Sidney Sussex College, Cambridge.

blood in England, in the vain attempt to conciliate Spain—as evidenced by the murder of Raleigh—were warnings that could not be disregarded by the leaders of the Puritan party.

The Puritan cause was necessarily the cause of liberty, and Oliver grew up to manhood while the contest between the opposing forces was slowly culminating in the dominating influence of Laud and 'the Romanising party.

Oliver was a member of the Parliament of 1628 which passed the Petition of Right, and under which England, for the first time, became subject to Parliamentary government. With these alarming portents rising before him, it is hardly to be wondered at that Charles should determine to resort to personal rule, and for the next eleven years (1629-40) the Star Chamber, with Laud as its director and ruling spirit, superseded Parliament. Under this priestly rule, Puritan ears were cropped and their bodies imprisoned, and the lesson was not likely to be lost upon the moody Puritan recluse at Ely. The entire experience of his own life and the experience of the two preceding generations, had given Oliver good cause to look upon Roman Catholic priests as traitors to Protestant England—as emissaries of a Power which was continually endeavouring to array every Popish interest against it—and as the most insidious and deadly enemies of civil and religious liberty. And, although Laud and Charles would not admit it, history has shown that the Puritans rightly judged that it was towards Rome, with its system of political and religious tyranny, that they were steadily marching.

It was with this strong conviction that Oliver sailed to reconquer Ireland, and to avenge the bloody massacres of the Protestant settlers, knowing full well that there would be no peace until England's authority was firmly re-established there.

" By the execution of the King the whole situation was changed. What had been a Rebellion under legal forms, became a real Revolution; in the room of the Parliament men saw a Council of State; in the room of a Monarchy, a Commonwealth ; and Cromwell was left the one commanding person on either side.

. . .  "Thus from the day when the King's head fell at Whitehall until the day of his own death there, nearly ten years later, Oliver Cromwell was the acknowledged master of England.

. . .  " The King being dead, the throne itself destroyed, and the three Estates of the Realm suppressed, a Dictator became inevitable.   And there was but one possible Dictator.   . . .

" The condition of England without was, however, for the moment more pressing even than her condition within.   The new Republic was not recognised by foreign sovereigns.   Its enemies were upheld and its agents were insulted throughout Europe. The bond that had held together the three kingdoms was dissolved.   Scotland proclaimed Prince Charles as king.   The contending factions in Ireland were at last united by the execution of Charles ; Rupert was there with a fleet ; and except for a few hard pressed garrisons, Ireland was now an independent and hostile country.  .  .  .   The preparations for the reconquest of Ireland were all made on a large and careful scale. But a pressing danger had first to be dealt with." *

The Army was in a state of mutiny, arising from many causes, and Oliver was not the man to parley with mutiny. "I tell you, sir," he said at the Council, "you have no other way to deal with these men but to break them to pieces, *or they will break us.*" There were three great outbursts, and Oliver dealt with them all, and by a mixture of promptness, sternness and sympathy, he quickly subdued the mutiny at the cost of only four lives.

**Milton, Latin** "Five months were occupied in the **Secretary.** preparation for this distant and difficult campaign. Cromwell's nomination was on the 15th March, 1649. On the same day Milton was appointed Latin Secretary to the Council. During April Cromwell arranged the marriage of his eldest son with the daughter of a very quiet, unambitious squire. . . . At length all was ready, and he set sail on the 13th August, with 9,000 men in about 100 ships. He was invested with supreme civil as well as military command in Ireland ; amply supplied with material and a fleet. Ireton, his son-in-law, was his second in command." †

**Cromwell in** Rarely has a military commander **Ireland, 1649.** found himself in a more difficult situation than that which confronted Oliver on his landing in Ireland on the 15th August, 1649.

Practically, the only portions of that country firmly held for the Parliament were the cities of Derry and Dublin, and the former was at the moment closely besieged, while Dublin itself had only

* F. Harrison. † Ibid.

recently been freed from the grip of the Irish levies.
But it was with Oliver, as with all great men; his
spirit and determination rose and increased with the
contemplation of the difficulties in front of him.

And if he needed any stimulus in carrying out the
task with which he was entrusted, the condition in
which he had left England and Scotland furnished
an abundant supply. The Scottish Royalists were
making tremendous efforts on behalf of the new king,
and all over England Charles's friends were ready to
support them by fomenting risings in every quarter.
" *Cromwell, we have need of thee,*" was felt by all the
friends of Liberty, for indeed the very life of the
Commonwealth depended upon his making short
work of his Irish commission.

Oliver landed in Dublin amidst scenes of the
wildest enthusiasm, for his coming was the presage of
a speedy triumph for the Protestant cause. On his
way to the Castle, he addressed the people, telling
them that " *by Divine Providence, he should restore
them all to their just liberties, and properties.*" His
very presence caused discordant elements in the
garrison to unite, and his confidence inspirited
the most timid.

He relieved the Protestants of Dublin from their
taxes, and a number of gentlemen volunteered as his
bodyguard at their own charge. " Inquiry showed
that Jones's Army, though it had fought well, had
very different manners from the Ironsides, and
especially much laxer notions on the subject of
plunder. The Lord-Lieutenant, therefore, issued a
declaration as to the principles upon which he
intended to conduct the war. He was resolved, 'by

the grace of God, diligently and strictly to restrain
such wickedness for the future.' He would have no
wrong or violence of any kind toward people of the
country, unless actually in arms or employed with
the enemy. He offered a free and secure market,
and promised safety to all persons disposed to pursue
their industry peaceably under protection of his Army.
Soldiers were warned that disobedience on these
points would be visited severely."*

**Marquis of**   Lord Ormonde was nominally in
**Ormonde.**   command of the Irish forces opposed
to Cromwell, but in reality they commanded him,
for they were composed mainly of Roman Catholics
of the most extreme sort. The minority was
made up of English Royalists, set free by the
conclusion of the war in England, and by
Presbyterians from the province of Ulster. These
latter were alarmed and disgusted by the facility
with which Ormonde yielded to the insatiable
demands of the Catholics—concessions which he
was powerless to withhold. The friction became
so great that the Ulster men were in more
danger from their allies than from Cromwell's
army. Little wonder, therefore, that they prepared
to make terms with the Lord-Lieutenant.

Accordingly, on the 26th April, 1650, a deputation,
consisting of Sir Robert Sterling, Mr. Michael Boyle,
Dean of Cloyne, and Colonel John Daniell, representing the Protestant Royalists serving under Lord
Inchiquin, had audience of Cromwell, and signed
articles agreeing to his conditions, which permitted
them to sell their movable property (except arms and

* Picton's *Cromwell.*

ammunition), and to retire to any part of Ireland under the authority of Parliament with passes, which should secure them from interference so long as they continued to act peaceably and in conformity with the conditions agreed upon.*

This was a great stroke of policy on the part of Oliver, for it had all the advantages of a victorious engagement without its risks and certain losses, and it helped materially to clear the way for his return to England, where his presence was urgently required.

The fearful cruelties and massacres which had been inflicted upon the English settlers by the Irish had roused such a spirit of exasperation and anger amongst Oliver's soldiers that it was certain that when it came to "push of pike" with the enemy, there would be terrible work.

Drogheda (Tredagh) and Wexford were stormed and sacked, and their garrisons—refusing to sur-render—put to the sword. Oliver's warmest admirers find it difficult to justify this extreme severity.

The war was "short, sharp and decisive," and large as the number of killed was, there is no doubt that it would have been much larger if Oliver had adopted less energetic measures, and suffered the conflict to linger on for another year.

Oliver leaves    In January, Parliament informed
Ireland, May,    Cromwell that they wished him to
1650.    return forthwith, but owing to con-
trary winds the message failed to reach him for two months, and as he was then engaged in active operations, he desired to remain until they were

* From the original documents in the Author's collection.

closed ; but in April Parliament despatched a frigate to "attend his pleasure," and at the end of May he went on board, leaving Ireton in chief command and his second son, Henry, in an unofficial capacity in Dublin.

The lurid character of the Irish campaign has somewhat obscured the circumstances under which Oliver left England.

The Second Civil War had only just ended, the King was dead, and a complete revolution effected. No settled government had taken the place of the old monarchy, and clearly the strongest and best men were wanted in London while orderly rule was being established.

It seems clear, too, that having become the foremost man in the country, Oliver would not have consented to leave England for an indefinite period and on a desperate enterprise, while everything was in a formative state, had he been the ambitious plotter described by his enemies. Napoleon returning, under somewhat similar circumstances, from his preliminary victories with his mind already fixed on empire, took care to remain in Paris while order was being evolved out of chaos ; "Cromwell had gone to Ireland, at imminent risk to his cause, to recover it to the Parliament in the shortest possible time, and with a relatively small army. He had gone there first to punish what was believed to have been a wholesale massacre and a social revolution ; to restore the Irish soil to England, and to replace the Protestant ascendancy. In the view of the Commonwealth government, the Mass was by law a crime, Catholic priests were legally outlaws, and all who resisted the Parliament were constructively guilty of murder and rebellion. Such were the accepted axioms of the whole Puritan party, and of Cromwell as much as any man."

. . . " For soldiers he found a new career. By a stroke of profound policy he encouraged foreign embassies to enlist Irish volunteers, giving them a free pass abroad. And thus it is said, some 40,000 Irishmen ultimately passed into the service of foreign sovereigns."

This may have been a " stroke of profound policy " at the time, but it bore bitter fruit for England during the next hundred years in its wars with foreign countries, for the " Irish legion " was always our most formidable foe.

" With great energy and skill the Lord-Lieutenant set about the reorganisation of government in Ireland. A leading feature of this was the Cromwellian settlement afterwards carried out under the Protectorate, by which immense tracts of land in the provinces of Ulster, Munster and Leinster, were allotted to English settlers, and the landowners of Irish birth removed into Connaught."

. . . " Such was the basis of the famous ' Cromwellian Settlement,' by far the most thorough act in the long history of the conquest of Ireland ; by far the most wholesale effort to impose on Ireland the Protestant faith and English ascendancy. Wholesale and thorough, but not enough for its purpose. It failed like all the others ; did more, perhaps, than any other to bind Ireland to the Catholic Church, and to alienate Irishmen from the English rule." *

* F. Harrison.

OLIVER CROMWELL.
From a contemporary French print.

Oliver arrived in Bristol, after a tempestuous crossing, in the *President* frigate (not the *Protector !*)

**Oliver in London, 31st. May, 1650.** and was received with three salvoes of artillery, and great acclamation. On his way to London, he halted at Hounslow Heath, where many deputations awaited his coming ; the Lord Mayor and his Council, Lord Fairfax and his chief officers, and nearly all the Members of Parliament were there ; and on reaching Hyde Park the Trainbands met him and formed an escort to Whitehall and the Cockpit, his future home. As he passed Tyburn, the road being thronged with people, one said to him, " See what a multitude of people come to attend your triumph ! " Oliver, who never exhibited keen desire for popular applause, replied, with a smile, " *More would come to see me hanged !* "

On taking his seat in Parliament again, the formal thanks of the House were tendered him from the lips of the Speaker. The Cockpit, near to Whitehall, was allotted him as a State residence, and there was further discussion as to a settled income for his needs, but with indefinite conclusion.

In Scotland the Cavaliers and Royalist Presbyterians had helped the cause of the Parliament by quarrels amongst themselves, the latter insisting upon Prince Charles taking the Covenant, and in an evil hour for himself, Montrose drew the sword to cut the knot, for which he was hanged in Edinburgh.

Charles, however, subscribed to the Presbyterian demand, with the usual Stuart mental reservation, duly put into effect when he was firmly seated on the throne.

The Scotch could not forgive the suppression of Presbyterianism in England, and, Charles having now taken the Covenant, they determined to again invade England, resolving, after having conquered it, to re-establish their own form of public worship, and to seat Charles on the throne of his fathers.

**Lord=General Cromwell, 26th June, 1650.** On June 12th, Parliament appointed Fairfax and Cromwell to the command of an expedition to Scotland. But the former declined to serve, stating that he had scruples on the subject which prevented his doing so. In vain did Cromwell and the other great officers beg Fairfax to reconsider the matter—he would not yield, and on the 25th he sent in his resignation of the office of Lord-General, which was the next day conferred upon Cromwell.

Fairfax died in 1672. His wife, a Presbyterian, was always a Royalist, and it was often suspected that she conveyed information to the enemy. Fairfax was by no means enthusiastic in the cause of the Parliament, and it was with a sense of relief, both to himself and to the country, that he finally resigned his office into the strong hands of Cromwell.

Three days after his appointment to the chief command Oliver set out for the North. His sudden advance, fresh from the bloody campaign in Ireland, struck dismay into the Scotch border. He advanced along the coast cautiously, resting on his ships, whilst his opponent and old companion-in-arms at Marston, David Lesley, thought to wear him out by drawing him on, avoiding battle, and cutting off his supplies.

" It was a religious war, between two sects, each of which regarded the other as schismatics. Thus the English army entered Scotland consumed with zeal to fight it out to the last man in defence of the Commonwealth, and to 'live and die with their renowned General.'"

Lesley fell back on a strong position on the coast between Edinburgh and Leith, Oliver following, and trying in vain to force a battle. The weather was wet, his men fell ill, and things began to look serious; twice he advanced against the Scots in vain ; his men became discouraged, and he fell back on Dunbar. By a skilful manœuvre Lesley passed around the English army, planting himself on the Lammermuir hills, and effectually blocking the pass that led into England. Besides being so advantageously placed, the Scots army was twice as large as Oliver's, and was well supplied, while the English, as one of them wrote, were a "poor, scattered, hungry, discouraged army." They lay on a small promontory jutting out into the North Sea, their only base being their ships.

Oliver fully recognised the danger of his position, and wrote confidential letters to England preparing the authorities for the worst.

"Wherefore, whatever becomes of us, it will be well for you to get what forces you can together and the South to help what they can. The business nearly concerneth all good people. If yr. forces had been in readiness to have fallen upon the back of Copperspath it might have occasioned supplies to have come to us. But the only wise God knoweth what is best. All shall work for good. Our spirits are comfortable, praised be the Lord, though our present condition be as it is ; and, indeed, we have much hope in the Lord, of whose mercy we have had large experience." *

But he was not cast down, and his attendant, Harvey, wrote of him at that time : "He was a strong man in the dark perils of war, in the high places of the field ; hope shone in him like a pillar of fire, when it had gone out in all the others."

His main hope lay in the chance of Lesley making a mistake, and, to his great relief, this actually happened.

Thinking that Oliver was about to embark his army, the Scotch General determined to get between him and his ships. When Oliver saw this he exclaimed, "The Lord hath delivered them into our hands !" This was on the 2nd September, 1650.

"Lesley had drawn down his wing to the coast, hoping to surround and crush the English in the act, as he supposed, of embarkation. Cromwell's design was to hold the main Scotch army with his big guns, whilst he fell suddenly with his best troops on Lesley's right wing, and so to roll it back upon its centre. The night was wild and wet ; the moon covered with clouds. The English lay partly in tents ; the Scotch, on the open hill-sides, crouched for shelter in the soaked shocks of corn. Both armies rested on their arms, waiting eagerly for dawn ; and on both sides many gathered in companies and prayed aloud, and for the last time, to the God of Battles." †

* Letter CXXXIX.   Oliver to Sir A. Haselrig at Newcastle.
† F. Harrison.

At four in the morning, by the light of the moon, the English began to move ; at six, they advanced to

**Dunbar, 3rd Sept., 1650.** the charge with this word for that day : "*The Lord of Hosts.*" The big guns kept the main Scots army back, whose right wing, however, drove the English towards the sea; then Oliver ordered a flank charge of cavalry, supporting it with foot ; his troopers returned to the assault, drove back the enemy, and then, as Oliver says in his despatch to the Council, " After the first repulse, they were made by the Lord of Hosts as stubble to our swords." In less than an hour the battle was won. " They run ! They run ! I profess they run !" said Oliver, as he watched the effect of his troopers' charge. " The whole army broke and disappeared, flying in all directions : some south, some north.

" Just then over the eastern ocean burst the first gleam of the sun through the morning mist. And above the roar of the battle was heard the voice of the General : ' Let God arise, let His enemies be scattered.' Then, as the whole Scotch army fled in wild confusion, the Lord General made a halt ; steadying his men and firing them afresh for the pursuit, he sang the 117th Psalm : ' O praise the Lord, all ye nations, praise Him all ye people ; for His merciful kindness is great towards us, and the truth of the Lord endureth for ever. Praise ye the Lord.' " *

Immediately after the battle, Oliver issued this

PROCLAMATION :

" Forasmuch as I understand there are several soldiers of the enemy's army yet abiding in the Field,

* F. Harrison.

who by reason of their wounds could not march from thence, these are therefore to give notice to the Inhabitants of this Nation that they may and hereby have free liberty to repair to the Field aforesaid, and with their carts or in any other peaceable way, to carry away the said soldiers to such places as they shall think fit; provided they meddle not with or take away any of the Arms there, and all Officers and Soldiers are to take notice that the same is permitted. Given under my hand at Dunbar, 4 Sept., 1650.

"  OLIVER CROMWELL.

" To be proclaimed by beat of Drum."

Such was the battle of Dunbar, fought on a day that was henceforth to become famous for that and for other victories gained by Oliver, and also for Death's victory over himself. The Scotch army was completely routed and broken in pieces, the whole of the arms, both great and small, were taken, and, wonderful to relate, Oliver lost only two officers and twenty men. Over 200 colours were also taken.

The Dunbar medal—executed by Simon—was given to each officer and soldier ; on one side is shown the head of Cromwell, with an inscription giving the word for the day and the date of the battle, and on the other a view of the House of Commons. There are in my collection several of these rare medals.

# CHAPTER XII.

FROM Dunbar Oliver wrote to his wife, telling her he was growing an old man, and felt the infirmities of age marvellously stealing upon him.

> *"For my beloved wife, Elizabeth Cromwell,*
> *" at the 'Cockpit.' These :—*

" My Dearest,          *" Dunbar, 4th Sept., 1650.*

> *" I have not leisure to write much. But I could chide thee that in many of thy letters thou writest to me that I should not be unmindful of thee and thy little ones. Truly, if I love you not too well, I think I err not on the other hand much. Thou art dearer to me than any creature. Let that suffice.*
>
> *" The Lord hath showed us an exceeding mercy ; who can tell how great it is ? My weak faith hath been upheld.*
>
> *" I have been in my inward man marvellously supported, though I assure thee I grow an old man, and feel infirmities of age marvellously stealing upon me. Would my corruptions did as fast decrease. Pray on my behalf in the latter respect.*
>
> *" The particulars of our late success Harry Vane or Gilbert Pickering will impart to thee. My love to all dear friends,*     *" I rest thine,*
>
>          *" Oliver Cromwell."*

* Carlyle. Letter CXLIII.

177

Sending Lambert to occupy Edinburgh, he set himself the task of securing the country south of the Forth as far as the Clyde.

When Oliver arrived in Edinburgh he found that the "pulpits were empty," the Presbyterian ministers having gone "on strike," and taken up their abode at the Castle.

Oliver sent them a civil message, inviting them to return and offering them free liberty of preaching and full security ; but they declined. The services, therefore, were conducted by some of Oliver's chaplains, and, *scandalum magnatum*, by some of his troopers !

The Presbyterian ministers were greatly shocked at the proceeding, and complained to Cromwell that "men of mere civil place and employment should usurp the calling and employment of the ministry."

Against this scornful, dog-in-the-manger complaint, Oliver's soul rose in rebellion, and he replied, hotly enough : "Are you troubled that Christ is preached ? Is preaching so inclusive in your function ? Doth it scandalise the Reformed Kirks and Scotland in particular ? Is it against the Covenant ? Away with the Covenant if this be so. Where do you find in the Scripture a ground to warrant such an assertion that preaching is exclusively your function ? Though an approbation from men hath order in it, and may do well, yet he that hath no better warrant than that, hath none at all. I hope that He that ascended up on high, may give His gifts to whom He pleases."

Charles Second goes to Wor= cester, 1650=51. Charles II. was crowned at Scone on the 1st January, 1651, but being driven from one place to another, he at length resolved to make a dash into England. Cromwell desired nothing better, and making his disposition for securing the rest of Scotland, began his march south in pursuit.

As Charles marched on with his small and jaded army he called for recruits but obtained none, the country people flying and driving their cattle before them. Lord Derby raised a small force, which was quickly destroyed by Colonel Robert Lilburne, and Charles, finding himself in danger of being hemmed in, struck out for the south-west and got to Worcester. At the end of August Cromwell also arrived, and soon found himself at the head of 30,000 men— three times the number that were with the King. Charles held a strongly-fortified position to the west of the city, in the triangle formed by the two rivers, the Teme and Severn, and with Oliver as his opponent, the result was a foregone conclusion.

" From the 28th August till the 3rd September the batteries played on the city, the works drawing closer round it, and the besieged continually giving ground. At dawn on the 3rd September—his fortunate day—Cromwell ordered his final assault. 'This day twelve-month,' runs a despatch, 'was glorious at Dunbar, this day hath been glorious at Worcester. The word then was "*The Lord of Hosts,*" and so it was now ; and, indeed, the Lord of Hosts was wonderfully with us.' " *

The "Crowning Mercy," 3rd Sept., 1651. By building two bridges of boats, Cromwell destroyed Charles's river defences, and the King from his look-out on the cathedral tower, seeing how things were going, brought his men inside the city, closely

* F. Harrison.

followed by Cromwell. Far into the night desperate street fighting continued, until the overthrow was complete. Thousands lay dead on the field; 10,000 prisoners were taken; Hamilton, Derby, Lauderdale, Lesley, and Massey—all the leaders were captured. The loss of the victors was under 200 men. " The dimensions of this mercy," wrote Cromwell to the Speaker, "are above my thoughts. It is, for aught I know, a crowning mercy."

" The Royalist cause was utterly crushed out at Worcester. Oliver never again appeared in the field; and during his lifetime the sword was not drawn again in England."

The romantic story of Charles's escape to France is wonderfully well told in a work recently written by Mr. Allan Fea.*

Oliver was now, without doubt, the foremost man in the nation, and his march towards London was a continuous triumphal progress. At Acton he was met by the Speaker and a deputation from the House, by the Lord Mayor, and a number of the chief citizens. A further sum of £4,000 a year was voted to him, and Hampton Court Palace was given him as a residence.

**Oliver at Hampton Court, Dictator.**      " Thereby he was recognised by what remained of legal authority as practically Dictator. He was now at the height of his power and prestige; this, then, was the moment when a Bonaparte would have seized the vacant throne." † And had he been the ambitious man his enemies have represented him to have been, he would undoubtedly have done so. But, it was

* *The Flight of the King.* (London : John Lane, 1897.)
† F. Harrison.

remarked that he carried himself with affability and modesty, and betook himself to work as a simple member of the Council. There he laboured assiduously for nineteen months, nor on any single occasion did he bring himself conspicuously before the nation. He served on the standing Committees of the Admiralty, of Trade and Foreign Affairs, of Law, of the affairs of Ireland and Scotland, "and on many others." As Captain-General and semi-official Dictator, Oliver worked on at the administrative business of the Nation, accepting the shadowy authority of the remnant of the Long Parliament. It was only after an anxious interval of abortive attempts at a settled government that he began to take independent action. " Nineteen months elapsed after Worcester fight before he closed the Long Parliament ; it was two years and three months before he was named Protector." *

The Civil War being over and the Revolution complete, " the peril, which had given the Commonwealth its cohesion and mighty force, was at an end, and the various elements of which that force was composed were now free to insist on their differences." † It may be taken for granted that the majority of the nation preferred a monarchical form of government, and only desired that it should be shorn of its arbitrary powers, but the Commonwealth party, by their organisation and earnestness, possessed an enormous predominance in effective strength. The Army was the backbone of the party, and it was composed of the flower of the people, "men who were, and knew themselves to be, the natural leaders of the people." Scarcely, indeed,

* F. Harrison.                    † Ibid.

in history has moral and material force thus been concentrated in a body possessing intense political conviction and consummate military discipline.

Their " political ideas were few, but very definite, and held with intense tenacity ; religious freedom, orderly government, and the final abolition of the abuses for which Charles and Laud had died. In religion they were mainly Independent, desiring the widest liberty for themselves and others. What they wanted was Peace and a settled Government, so that they might return to their homes and to civil life." *

Parliament, or what was left of it, was fast getting back into the hands of the lawyers and Presbyterians. The business of the country was in great confusion from the breaking-up of the old order, and the neglect or inability of Parliament to proceed with much-needed legislation. The day after Dunbar Cromwell wrote to the Speaker as to the pressing needs of the country, saying : " Relieve the oppressed, hear the groans of poor prisoners in England. Be pleased to reform the abuses of all professions, *and if there be any one such that makes many poor to make a few rich, that suits not a Commonwealth.*" But Parliament would do nothing, spite of urgent entreaties and advice ; the Army and the country became intensely dissatisfied, and it was evident that a crisis was approaching.

Zbe Crisis,    The struggle had gone on during
1652.     the whole of 1652, Cromwell and his officers pressing the Parliament for needed reforms and for the calling of a new Parliament. Frequent conferences between the officers and leaders in Parliament were held, but without result, and Oliver's

* F. Harrison.

patience became exhausted. The Army and the people were weary of petitioning Parliament—the last petition of the former was a very noteworthy one, and full of practical suggestions. They asked for " a reform of legal procedure, redress of abuses in Excise, and they insisted on a more faithful observance of Articles of War granted to the enemy. They urged that the National revenues should all go into one treasury under officers appointed by Parliament, and that half-yearly accounts should be published. Finally, they asked once more that a new ' Representative ' should be appointed." The House complained of dictation on the part of their "servants," the Army, and appealed to Cromwell to rebuke them ; but he took the opposite course and approved their action.

It became clear that the Long Parliament—or rather the Rump of it—was about to come to an end. It had outlived its mandate, which was to curb the tyranny of the King, and that of the priests, which was even worse, and to ensure constitutional government. But the King was dead and his power destroyed, and new "forcers of conscience " had arisen in the place of Laud ; the Nation demanded reforms, but the fifty gentlemen now arrogating to themselves the title of Parliament were quite comfortable in their positions as supreme rulers of the country, and were slow to move ; indeed, Cromwell, on one occasion, charged them with taking three months to decide the meaning of the word "incumbrance,"—and he was about to give them a practical illustration of its meaning.

After repeated warnings from the Army and from prominent Republicans, Parliament agreed to pass an Act calling a new " Representative," but was careful to so frame it that they themselves should still remain in supreme power. The new Parliament was to consist of 400 members, but the Rump were to retain their seats without re-election, and were to be able to reject, at pleasure, newly elected members whose opinions were not favourable to them.

The artifice was too transparent ; it was obviously intended to perpetuate their own powers, and therefore could be no settlement at all.

"Cromwell thereupon called another Conference on the 19th April, 1653, at which Sir Harry Vane and about twenty other members attended. There he and the Generals told the Parliament men clearly that they would not suffer them to pass such a Bill. They proposed, as an alternative, a commission of forty leading men to summon a new Parliament. The sitting ended late at night without a decision, it being agreed to meet again the next day, with an understanding that in the meantime the Bill should not be passed."

The next day the Conference was renewed, but while it was proceeding word was brought that the House was hastily passing the proposed measure through all its stages at one sitting. Furious at what he believed to be the bad faith of Vane and the leaders, Cromwell called a company of musketeers to attend him, and with Lambert and other officers strode silently to the House.

The scene which ensued is a very familiar one to all readers of history, and is well described by Harrison.

"**Sir Harry Vane, Sir Harry Vane!**" Oliver took his seat while Vane was pressing the House to pass the Dissolution Bill without delay and without the customary forms. Then, getting up, he began to tell them of their shortcomings, accused them of intention to perpetuate themselves in power ; and rising into passion, he told them that the Lord had done with them, and had chosen other instruments to carry on His work. A member rising to complain of such language coming from "a trusted servant," Oliver was roused to fury, and leaving his seat, walked up and down the floor of the House, stamping with his feet and crying, "You are no Parliament, I say you are no Parliament. Come, come, we have had enough of this ; I will put an end to your prating. Call them in." Twenty or thirty musketeers marched in, while the rest of the guard were placed at the doors and in the lobby.

Vane, from his place, cried out, "This is not honest, yea, it is against morality and common honesty." But he had nothing to say about his own lack of honesty in failing to keep the promise of the previous day, and so Oliver turned on him, with a loud voice, "O Sir Harry Vane, Sir Harry Vane, the Lord deliver me from Sir Harry Vane !" And then, pointing to various members, he accused them of lacking public and private morality. Going up to the table, and pointing to the mace, he said, "What shall we do with this bauble ?   Here, take it away !" and gave it to a musketeer. "Fetch him down," he cried to Harrison, pointing to the Speaker. Lenthall refused to come down unless by force. "Sir," said Harrison, "I will lend you my hand," and putting his hand within his, the Speaker came down.

The members went out, fifty-three in all, Cromwell speaking in loud tones. To Vane he said that he might have prevented this, but that he was a juggler and was wanting in common honesty. And then, snatching the Bill of Dissolution from the hand of the Clerk, he put it under his cloak, and ordering the guards to clear the House and to lock it up, went away to Whitehall.

And thus closed one of the most remarkable passages in the history of England.

In considering Cromwell's act, it should be borne in mind that while the germ and semblance of legal authority remained with the Parliament, it was, in reality, as much a revolutionary body as Oliver and his Council of Officers ; but while the latter demanded the reform of abuses, the Parliament wasted its time in frivolous debates.

Everything was in confusion, "the law in especial manner was in a state of chaos. There were 23,000 unheard cases waiting in Chancery, and this was a perpetual grievance both to the General and his soldiers. It might surprise us to find the Army and its chief so constantly troubled about the abuses of the law, did we not remember that the Civil War was the turning point in the history of English law ; that it shattered the whole system of feudal tenure, and with the Restoration we find the land law mainly what it continued to be down to the present century. The period of transition was in times of chaos and injustice, and Cromwell and his Ironsides were men to whom social injustice and official tyranny never appealed in vain. But, besides the law, practical questions had to be solved. An army of 50,000 men had to be reduced to one half, and a mass of diseased and wretched prisoners had to be disposed of ; * and fortresses and castles dismantled, reduced, or repaired. Ireland and Scotland had to be brought into permanent settlement. In one word, a nation which had been torn by the years of desperate civil war, and of which every institution had been passing through a crisis, lay waiting for order, settlement and reorganisation." †

Parliament being dissolved, all committees, including the Council of State, naturally ceased to exist. Three days later appeared the " Declaration of the Lord General and his Council of Officers." In it the state of affairs was referred to and his own action justified ; all judges, sheriffs, mayors and other officials were requested to continue to administer their offices.

* The following letter (in the Author's collection) from Sir F. Willoughby, addressed " ffor his Honored ffrind Robert Blackbourne Esq^e Secretary to the Comp^y for y^e Admiralty and Navy these present Whitehall," refers to this state of things:

" There was in y^e time of y^e fleete being at Portsmouth in Aprill last a great number of sick & wounded men sett ashore and there being nobody to look after them I was constrayned to make use of my brother to take care of y^t business."

Sir F. W. then goes on to say that the Committee refused to recognise his brother's claim without a certificate, and that his brother took great pains to ensure a speedy recovery of the men, and " hazarded himselfe, going amongst men y^t had y^e smaule pox & spotted fevour, by which meanes (instrumentally) he gott a sickness y^t had neere cost him his life. All the phisitiones giving him over for a dead man.

" 20 Dec^r 1653."

(A few days after Oliver's first installation as Protector.)

† F. Harrison.

"Within a few days came in declarations of adhesion from the navy, the armies in Scotland and Ireland, and addresses from municipal and civic bodies. There were no resignations, no arrests, and no further force. The fighting men approved, the officials obeyed, and the nation acquiesced. And without a show of opposition, the whole machinery of the State passed quietly into the strong hand of Cromwell." (F. Harrison.)

**The Little Parliament, 4th July, 1653.** One of his first acts was to call a Parliament, which met on the 4th July, 1653, about 140 members being present. In his opening speech, Cromwell said that he was anxious to "divest the sword of all power in the civil administration, and had summoned them that he might devolve the burden on their shoulders." This was the Little Parliament ; it sat for five months —a set of "godly men," but utterly unpractical, the majority of them being at length very glad to place their resignations in the General's hands, leaving him the sole legalised authority in the State.

**Oliver, Lord Protector, 16th Dec., 1653.** He immediately summoned his Council of Officers and other persons of interest, and in a few days it was announced that the Council had offered, and he had accepted, the "style of Lord Protector of the Commonwealth," to carry on the Government by the advice of a Council and with an Instrument of Government, or written constitution. The government was invested in a Protector and Council, and in the Commons of England, Scotland, and Ireland, meeting in triennial Parliaments ; the first to begin on the 3rd September, 1654. Until the sitting

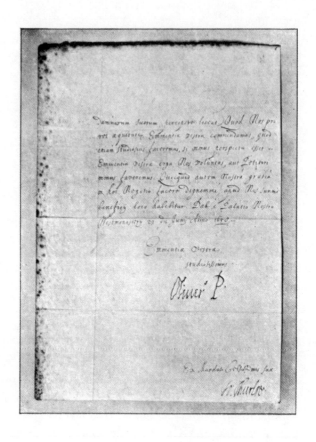

**LETTER (PORTION OF) FROM "OLIVER P." TO CARDINAL MAZARIN.**

Written by JOHN MILTON, signed by Oliver, and countersigned by
Thurloe, Secretary of State.

This letter is dated 23rd June, Anno. 1658, just ten weeks before the
Protector's death (see Addenda).

From the original, in the Author's Collection.

of Parliament the Protector and his Council had power to make ordinances having the force of law. The office of Protector was to be elective, and he was to be chosen by the Council.

Oliver was installed as Protector on the 16th of December, 1653—thus becoming a constitutional and strictly limited sovereign.

"From his installation to his death, Oliver held supreme power as Protector of the Commonwealth. His task now was to control the Revolution which he had led to victory; and his career enters on a new and greater phase. He stands out amongst the very few men in all history who, having overthrown an ancient system of government, have proved themselves with even greater success to be constructive and conservative statesmen." *

Oliver was aided in his great task by many noble men; "he had with him the Puritan rank and file, the great majority of the superior officers; such clear and lofty spirits as those of Milton and Marvell, Blake and Lockhart, Lawrence and Lisle; the men of business; all moderate men of every party who desired peace, order, good government; the great cities; the army and navy. With these and his own commanding genius, he held his own triumphantly; slowly winning the confidence of the nation by virtue of his unbroken success and (as it seemed) miraculous fortune. Thus he grew ever larger, until he lay in his last sleep, murmuring, 'my work is done'; as in battle, a soldier who had never met with a reverse, so a statesman, who, in a supreme place, had never met with a fall." †

* F. Harrison.   † Ibid.

But he had against him the Republicans, "to whom the Revolution meant republican equality more than liberty, and legal right even more than order and prosperity." * Every man with a "fad" was against Oliver, the Bible fanatic, who wanted to rule England as Joshua ruled Israel, the Constitutional martinets and the socialist dreamers. These were all against him from the first.

His disputes with his Parliaments all hinged upon the point as to whether the Executive power should be at the disposal of Parliament, as the result of a hostile vote ; this he would have none of.

" From first to last, after the closing of the Long Parliament, he struggled for five years to realise his fixed idea of a dual Government—neither a Dictator without a Parliament, nor a Parliament without a head of the Executive. With dogged iteration he repeats—the government shall rest with a single person and a Parliament, the Parliament making all laws, and voting all supplies, co-ordinate with the authority of the chief person, and not meddling with the Executive. This was his idea—an idea which the people of England have rejected, but which the people of America have adopted. More than a century later the founders of the United States revived and established Oliver's ideal, basing it upon popular election, a thing which, in 1654, was impossible in England." †

Oliver's intense dislike of Dictatorship—an office forced upon him by circumstances—and his longing for a settled constitutional Government, are clearly shown in the concluding chapters of Frederic

* F. Harrison.   † Ibid.

Harrison's admirable *Life*. But "he was no Parliamentary leader, and never could become one. His scorn of eloquent egoism, his hatred of obstruction, delay, and waste, his intense masterfulness and passion for action, made him unfit for Parliamentary work.

"The fixed idea of Cromwell was the fixed idea of the founders of the United States of America. There should be, he thought, a written Instrument; there should be an Executive authority, not directly subordinate to Parliament; and there should be what Oliver called 'fundamentals,' — fundamental bases not alterable like ordinary laws.

"In his Council and offices were some of the ablest men who have ever served this country. But the glory of his rule is John Milton. The first political genius of his age was served by the greatest literary genius of the time."

Cromwell and Milton. During the struggle with the Long Parliament Milton wrote his famous sonnet, "Cromwell, our chief of men." It was upon the establishment of the Protectorate that he published the magnificent panegyric in the *Defensio Secunda* :—

"*We are deserted, Cromwell, you alone remain; the sum total of our affairs has come back to you and hangs on you alone; we all yield to your insuperable worth.* . . . *In human society there is nothing more pleasing to God, more agreeable to Reason, nothing fairer and more useful to the State, than that the worthiest should bear rule.*"

Amid all the cares of government, Oliver was not unmindful of the claims of literature and learning. He was a liberal patron of the University of Oxford when Chancellor, and he directed the application of monies derived from the church lands in Scotland to aid the revenues of King James's College in Edinburgh ; and the College at Glasgow largely benefited by his good offices. Like other members of his family, Oliver was evidently fond of music ; nor do his tastes in that respect appear to have been confined to the severe, if not grim, school represented by the old Sternhold and Hopkins psalm tunes, if we may judge from the interesting and curious collection of MS. songs, corantos, masques, galliards, and other pieces compiled by his cousin, Anne Cromwell.*

When King Charles was in Scotland, in 1633, he promised to give £200 to the Glasgow College, but, like many other royal promises, it was forgotten, and it remained for the Protector to redeem the good name of the dead king, for Oliver paid the money in 1654.

Oliver issued his warrant for the founding of the University of Durham, directing that the revenue should be provided out of the funds of the Bishop and Chapter; but the intentions of the Protector were temporarily frustrated by the jealousy of the Universities of Oxford and Cambridge, the authorities of these institutions declaring that the State did not require a third University, and that its establishment would interfere with their vested rights of conferring degrees.

Oliver also conferred a rich boon upon all succeeding generations by causing Richmond Park to be thrown open to the public for ever.

* Vide Addenda.

EQUESTRIAN PORTRAIT OF OLIVER, LORD PROTECTOR.
From a rare silver plaque in the Author's Collection.

# CHAPTER XIII.

**Oliver's first Parliament, 3rd, Sept., 1654.** OLIVER'S first Protectorate Parliament met on the 3rd September, 1654, the writs of course being in his name.

Instead of proceeding with the business of the nation, the Parliament, under the leadership of Haselrig, Bradshaw, and other republicans, began at once to question the very Instrument of Government under which they sat. This, Oliver would not stand ; on the 12th September he again summoned the House to meet him, and addressed them in a powerful speech :—

" They were," he said, " a free Parliament, provided they recognised the authority which had called them together. I called not myself to this place ! God and the People of these nations have borne testimony to it. God and the People shall take it from me, else I will not part with it. I should be false to the trust which God hath placed in me, and to the interest of the people of these nations, if I did."

**First Parliament dissolved 22nd Jan., 1655=6.** The Parliament continued to disregard the authority of the Protector ; at the end of five months they had not sent up a single act for his assent, neither had they provided supply. On the 22nd of January, 1655, Oliver dissolved Parliament in a speech full of reproaches.

On the 17th of September, 1656, Oliver called
his last Parliament, having ruled the country through
his Major Generals during the twenty months that
**Second Parlia=** had elapsed since the previous one.
**ment, 17th** These men, by their arbitrary acts,
**Sept., 1656.** had stirred up a feeling of discontent
and unrest throughout the land, thereby bringing the
Protector's Government into the greatest disrepute.

When old Sir Jacob Astley surrendered his sword
after his defeat at Stow-in-the-Wold in the final
action of the first Civil War, he said to his captors,
*"My masters, you have done your work and may go
play, unless you please now to fall out among yourselves."*

The "falling out" had now commenced in earnest,
the country was distracted by contending factions,
and Oliver was at his wits' end.

His great desire was to see a Parliament
brought together which should be composed of good
business men, well affected to the new order of
things, who would devote themselves to putting an
end to the existing distractions which were threatening the life of the Government. But in spite of all
precautions more than one hundred rabid malcon-
tents were returned, and were promptly rejected by
the Council.

This Parliament concerned itself principally with a
scheme for vesting the Crown in Oliver, a majority
of the members being in favour of that course. The
country was by no means averse to the proposal, and
it was actively supported by the lawyers and business
men, as well as the more conservative of the Puritans ;
but the bulk of the Army disliked it, and the various
fanatics were rabidly antagonistic.

Twice the Parliament implored the Protector to accept the Kingship, but after much consideration he finally refused it. His enemies, both Republican and Royalist—and he had about as many enemies as any man ever had—were in entire agreement on one point, at any rate : they all believed he desired the Kingship, but that he let "I dare not wait upon I would."

Replying to an urgent request that he should assume the title, he declared that he valued it "but as a feather in his hat." He knew that he possessed supreme power, and that was enough for him ; but he also knew that six hundred years of unbroken kingship had permeated every institution in the land. It was known to the law, to the constitution, and to the people, and its prerogatives and rights were settled by custom. He felt, too, that while the " King" was to the people at large the outward and visible sign of authority, a " Protector " was but a *locum tenens*—an unfamiliar makeshift. Moreover, Cromwell never forgot that the great object of the war had been, not the abolition of monarchy, but the limitation of its powers.

To all unbiassed students of his career, one fact stands out in clear relief—he was the most conservative of revolutionists. It is equally clear that it was due to Charles much more than to Oliver that the kingly office was abolished.

Cromwell did his utmost to persuade Charles to adopt constitutional government ; indeed, to such a point did he carry his efforts, that many of his colleagues began to suspect his loyalty to "the cause," and it was not until he was convinced, by proof upon proof, of the King's extreme duplicity and utter untrustworthiness, that he threw in his lot with the Republican party in the Army and country.

The Parliament, finding itself unable to persuade Oliver to accept the kingly title, proceeded to make him sovereign in all but name.

**The Hereditary Protectorate, 26th June, 1657.** The first Protectorate ended in 1657, and on the 26th of June of that year Oliver was installed in the office for the second time with all the pomp and circumstance of a royal coronation. His powers were also extended, enabling him to name his successor, and to summon a "Second House" of Parliament.

In my collection are two copies of the very rare document by which the second appointment of the Protector was proclaimed; it is styled, "A Proclamation by his Highness and Parliament," and is dated at Westminster the 26th day of June, 1657. The Proclamation is ordered to be "forthwith published in the City of London and the respective cities, counties, corporations, and market towns, to this end that none may have cause to pretend ignorance in this behalf."

**Oliver's "Lords" and Commons meet, Jan. 20, 1657=8.** After the Installation, Parliament adjourned until the 17th September, and then further adjourned to the 20th January, 1657-8. In the meantime, in pursuance of the provision for summoning "another house," writs were issued to 56 gentlemen out of the 70 authorised by the *Petition* and *Advice* (suitable persons not yet having been found to complete the number) and Parliament was duly opened by the Protector—both

# A PROCLAMATION
### BY
## His Highnes and the Parliament.

Whereas the Knights, Citizens, and Burgesses of the Parliament of England, Scotland and Ireland, taking into their consideration, the duty incumbent upon them, to provide for the future Peace and Settlement of the Government of these Nations, according to the Laws and Customes of the same, by their humble Petition and advice, have presented their desires unto his Highnes Oliver Lord Protector, that He would by and under the Name and Stile of Lord Protector, of the Commonwealth of England, Scotland, and Ireland, and the Dominions and Territories thereunto belonging, Hold, and Exercise the Office of Chief Magistrate of these Nations: Whereunto the Lord Protector, upon due and mature Consideration of the said Petition and Advice, hath consented: And his Highnes the Lord Protector and the Parliament, judging it necessary, that publication be made of the Premisses; Have thought meet, and do hereby strictly Charge and Command all and every person and persons, of what Quality and Condition soever, in any of the said three Nations, to take notice of the Premisses, and to conform and submit themselves unto the Government so established. And the Lord Mayor of the City of London, and all Sheriffs, Mayors, Bayliffs, and other Publick Ministers and Officers, whom this may concern, are required to cause this Proclamation, together with the said Petition and Advice, to be forthwith Published in the City of London, and the respective Counties, Cities, Corporations and Market-Towns, to the end that none may have cause to pretend ignorance in this behalf.

Given at Westminster the 26. day of June, 1657.

THE SECOND INSTALLATION OF OLIVER, AS PROTECTOR, 26th JUNE, 1657.
From a scarce original in the Author's Collection.

Houses being present. Here is an account of the
opening ceremony, reproduced from a hitherto unpublished document—*The Journal of Oliver's House
of Lords* :* "His Highnes being set in his Chayre

* From a MS. Journal of Oliver's House of Lords, in the
Author's collection. In a communication from the British
Museum (where the volume had been sent for inspection) it
is stated : "The Journal of the Protectorate House of Lords
appears to be of great importance. So far as I can discover,
no other copy of this Journal exists, and, according to the
Parliamentary History, vol. xxi., 1763, p. 263, 'there are
no records left us of their Proceedings, except what the
Journal of the Commons supply.' "

In a letter under date, Westminster, 24th March, 1659-60
from John Maidston, personal friend of Oliver, and Treasurer
to the Protector Richard, after referring to Oliver's second
Installation as Protector, in 1657, under the "Petition and
Advice," occurs this passage :

"In it (the 'Petition and Advice') provision was made for
another House of Parliament, instead of the old Lords ; that
this might be a screen or balance betwixt the Protector and
Commons, as the former lords had been betwixt the King
and them. These to consist of 70 persons, all at first to be
nominated by the Protector, and, after, as any one died, a
new one to be nominated by him and his successors, and
assented to by themselves, or without that consent, not to
sit : twenty of them was a quorum. It was no small task for
the Protector to find 'idoneous' men for this place, because
the future security of the honest interest seemed to be laid
up in them . . . . for they would propagate their own
kind as a single person (i.e. Protector) could not . . . so
barren was the island of persons of quality, spirited for such
a service, as they were not to be found . . . . This
forced him to make it up of men of mean rank, and consequently of less interest, and upon trial, too light for balance,
too thin for a screen . . . . being made a scorn by the
nobility and gentry, and generality of the people ; the House
of Commons continually spurning at their power, and spending large debates in controverting their title, till at length
the Protector dissolved the Parliament, and so silenced that
controversy for that time."—Thurloe, vol. i. p. 766.

Maidston in writing of Oliver's Lords quoted 1 Cor. i. 26 v.
"Ye see your calling, *not many wise nor noble.*"

of State, and the Lords sitting in their places, the Howse of Com͠ons were sent for, and being come with their Speaker to the Barre, His Highness spake to them to this effect—(Here enter speech)

"Then the Lord Com^r Fyennes standing by the [chair of] State on the right hand made a speach to the effect following

(not entered) *

"Which being ended the Com͠ons w^th their Speaker retorned vnto their house and his Highness departed.

"Ordered that all the members of this house who haue not this day delivered in their writts of Sum͠ons doe bring them into the house tomorrow or as soone as they may to the end an entry of them may be made by the Clerke and then the same to be retorned.

"The Lord Com^r Fyennes by direccon of the house declared this present Parliam^t to be continued till tomorrow nine of the Clock in the morning."

The Commons, on reassembling under the New Constitution, readmitted the excluded members, Haselrig and others, having no longer power to reject any who were willing to take the prescribed oath. These men, from their experience and ability, soon became the leaders of the House, and again commenced their old tactics by endeavouring to destroy the Constitution under which they had met.

---

* The " *Journal* " was evidently the Clerk's rough copy, and doubtless the speeches were to have been entered in the fair copy, which appears not to have been made.

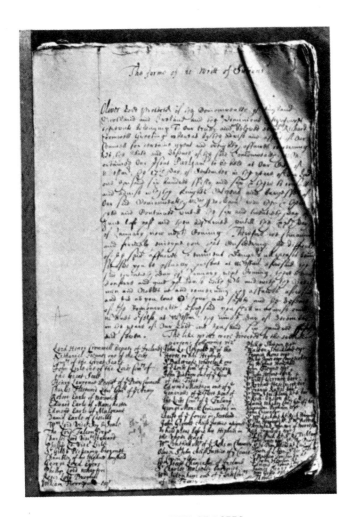

OLIVER'S HOUSE OF LORDS.

THE WRIT OF SUMMONS, WITH A COMPLETE LIST OF OLIVER'S "LORDS."
From the only known copy of the Journal of the Protectoral House of Lords.
In the Author's Collection.

Oliver had aroused the susceptibilities of the Republican members of the Commons, by referring to the "other house" as "the Lords," and when that House sent a message to the Commons, proposing the setting apart of a day for a solemn fast, a heated discussion ensued, causing all other business to be set aside.

It was more than Oliver could bear. Suffering from illness, and from grave anxiety on account of the dissatisfaction in the Army—with Royalist plots making head in all directions—it was maddening to him that his last hope of a constitutional settlement of the Government should be shattered by the "irresponsible chatter" of doctrinaires, and the malice of personal enemies in the House of Commons.

Summoning the two Houses into his presence, he suddenly dissolved Parliament in a speech of burning indignation and proud defiance, calling upon God to judge between them and him.

Such was Oliver's last Parliament.

"Apart from opposition from his Parliament, the Protectorate was one unbroken success. Order, trade, justice, learning, culture, rest and public confidence returned and grew ever stronger . . . . and with these, a self-respect, a spirit of hope and expansion such as had not been felt since the defeat of the Armada. But it was in foreign policy that the splendour of Oliver's rule dazzled his contemporaries." "His greatness at home," wrote Clarendon, "was but a shadow of the glory he had abroad." It was the epoch when supremacy at sea finally passed from the Dutch to the English ; it was the beginning of the maritime empire of England.

" Never had the fortunes of ' the cause ' stood firmer than in July, 1658, had but Oliver been destined to live out his three score years and ten. At home, rebellion and plots had been once more utterly stamped out ; abroad, the capture of Dunkirk had raised the glory of England to its highest point ; a new Parliament was preparing, it was hoped, with happier prospects.

" But the wings of the Angel of Death already were hovering over the house of Oliver.

" His youngest daughter, Frances, a bride of three months, was made a widow in February, by the death of young Rich, grandson and heir to the Earl of Warwick.   The old Earl, the staunchest friend of the Protector amongst the Peers, followed his grandson in April.   Next, in July, the Protector's favourite daughter, Elizabeth Claypole, lay dying at Hampton Court.   She, too, had recently lost her youngest boy, Oliver.   Through nearly the whole of July the broken-hearted father hung over her bedside, unable to attend to any public business whatever. On the 6th of August she was dead.   Oliver himself had sickened during her last days, and although he came to London on the 10th, when she was buried in Henry VII's Chapel, he returned to Hampton Court very ill."   His physicians, thinking that the air of Whitehall might be more favourable for his ailment, Oliver was removed there on the 24th.   It was his last journey, for " his time was come, and neither prayers nor tears could prevail with God to lengthen out his life."

" ' On Monday, the 30th of August, there raged a terrific storm, and superstition and party malice made the most of it.'

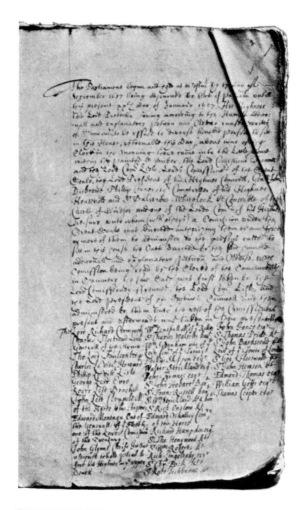

ADJOURNMENT OF PARLIAMENT FROM 17TH SEPTEMBER, 1657,
TO 20TH JANUARY, 1657-58.

From the MS. Journal of the House of Lords.
In the Author's Collection.

" The dying man was now conscious only partially and at intervals. They urged him to name his successor. The sealed paper with Richard's name in it could not be found. Was it Richard ? No man now knows. Twice the sinking ruler was believed to have given some indistinct assent." The night before his death he was very restless, speaking often to himself, "and there being something to drink offered him, he was desired to take the same and endeavour to sleep—unto which he answered : *'It is not my design to drink or sleep ; but my design is to make what haste I can to be gone.'* "

" Towards morning he used some expressions of consolation and peace, and some of deep humility and self-abasement.

**Death, 3rd Sept., 1658.** " The day that dawned was his day of triumph—the 3rd of September,— the day of Dunbar and Worcester. He was then speechless and remained all day in a stupor ; prayer, consternation and grief, all around him. Between three and four in the afternoon the watchers by his bedside heard a deep sigh. Oliver was dead."*

" *His ashes in a peaceful urn shall rest;*
*His name a great example stands to show*
*How strangely high endeavours may be blest,*
*Where Piety and Valour jointly go.*"†

Twenty-seven years after there was another death-bed scene at Whitehall. That anointed reprobate, Charles II., the hero of the " Blessed " Restoration, after a life of shameless profligacy, lay tossing on his bed of pain, complaining that he was a " most unconscionable long time in dying."

* F. Harrison.    † Dryden's *Panegyric.*

This man, who dared not look the Lion of England in the face while yet alive, and who was engaged in killing flies on the windows of his palace in the company of one of his mistresses, while the enemies of his country were sailing up the Thames, destroying the Royal ships; this man was guilty of the incredible meanness of causing the body of the Great Protector to be taken from its grave and hung on the gallows at Tyburn. And this is the record, as published in the newspapers of the day : " January 30th, 1660 o.s. The odious carcasses of O. Cromwell, H. Ireton, and J. Bradshaw drawn upon sledges to Tyburn, and being pulled out of their coffins, there hanged at the several angles of that triple tree till sunset. Then taken down, beheaded, and their loathsome trunks thrown into a deep hole under the gallowes. Their heads were afterwards set upon poles on the top of Westminster Hall." And this is the mason's receipt for taking up the corpses : " May, the 4th day, 1661. Received then in full of the worshipful Serjeant Norfolke, fourteen shillings for taking up the corps of Cromell, and Ierton and Brasaw. Recd. by mee, John Lewis."

In these days of Tory reaction and reassertion of clerical domination, when

" New foes arise
Threat'ning to bind our souls with secular chains "

—foes, reinforced by deserters from the Army of Progress—it becomes increasingly necessary that the motives which actuated the leaders of thought in the 17th century in their struggle against Tyranny, should be re-stated and made clear to the rising

THE DEATH MASK.

From a copy in the Author's Collection.

generation of Nonconformists and to Englishmen generally.

That the question is not one of merely academic interest is proved by the fact that although two and a half centuries have elapsed since the death of Oliver, the antagonism excited by the mention of his name is little less acute than in the days immediately following the " Blessed " Restoration. The spirit of Laud is still rampant in certain quarters ; and, although it is no longer possible to crop the ears of pestilent Nonconformists, it *is* still possible for bigoted and unscrupulous clergymen to harass and inflict grievous loss upon humble Nonconformists in numberless rural districts.

It is the continued existence of this spirit which imposes upon those who have suffered from its manifestation—as I have—the imperative duty of recalling to the minds of their children what their forefathers endured in their determination to secure the blessings of civil and religious liberty for succeeding generations. It has been well said by a recent writer, * " If Charles I. and Archbishop Laud had succeeded, the liberties of England would have perished, and the England of to-day would have been in the condition of Spain or Russia " ; and it is to Oliver Cromwell, more than to any other individual, that the English-speaking race are indebted for the boundless freedom that they now enjoy. He was the embodiment of the forces that for ever destroyed autocratic government in Church and State, in the persons of Charles and Laud, and he is aptly

* Dr. R. F. Horton. *Oliver Cromwell : A Study in Personal Religion.* (London : James Clarke & Co).

described by Dr. S. R. Gardiner as "the greatest, because the most typical Englishman of all time."

Well may Carlyle say : "*The memory of Oliver Cromwell, as I count, has a good many centuries in it.*"

BATTLE MAP OF THE CIVIL WAR.

RICHARD  CROMWELL.

RICHARD CROMWELL, PROTECTOR.

# CHAPTER XIV.

*" General Monck to the Sheriff of Renfrewshire.*

*" 10th Sept., 1658.*

*" Sir,*

*" Itt haveing pleased the most wise God in his provi-*
*dence to take out of this world that moste serene and*
*renouned Oliver, late Lord Protector, whose name and*
*memory will be ever pretiouse to all good men ; and his*
*said late Highness having in his lifetyme according to*
*the humble petition and advice, appointed and declared*
*the most noble and excellent lord, the Lord Richard,*
*eldest sonne of his said late highness, to succeed him in*
*the Government ; His highnes Councill heere have*
*therefore, by direction of the Privy Councill in England,*
*ordered the inclosed Proclamation to be published of*
*which they have sent you severall printed coppies heere*
*inclosed, that you may duly proclaime the same in your*
*Sheriffdoome ; and you are with all expedition to send*
*some of the said printed copies to the magistrates of*
*each burgh royall therein.*

*" Signed in the name, and by order, of the Councill.*

*" GEORGE MONCK.*

*" Edin. 10th September, 1658.*

*" For the High Sherriffe of the Shire of Renfrew, These,"*

In all ages the successors of great men have had
difficult *rôles* to play, and have suffered in reputation

much more than they would have done had they
been separated by a generation or two from their
great predecessors; and this is more particularly the
case when a distinguished man is succeeded by his
son. There have, of course, been exceptions, as in
the case of King Solomon, and of the younger Pitt,
but such exceptions may well be held to prove the
rule.

After making every allowance, however, for
Richard Cromwell as being "the son of his father,"
and after taking into account the unexampled difficulties of his position in the State at the demise of
his illustrious sire, it must be admitted that he was
entirely unequal to the great task which then
devolved upon him.

Like too many young men in every age, he
appears to have taken it for granted that the edifice
raised by the genius and untiring energy of his
father, must of necessity endure after its founder had
disappeared from the scene of his triumphs. But in
matters of State, as in the concerns of every-day life,
the truth remains that they can only be maintained
by the exercise of the same qualities that first
brought them into being.

Speculation has often been indulged in as to what
would have happened if the Great Protector had
named as his successor his second surviving son, the
Lord Lieutenant of Ireland; but all such speculations
are necessarily vain. It is true that Henry had been
engaged in affairs of State from early youth and had
evinced a great capacity for government; in Ireland
he had shown that he possessed in an eminent
degree one of the greatest qualities of a Statesman—

the *fortiter in re* and the *suaviter in modo*, but it is also true that the situation in England, at Oliver's death, demanded qualities which have rarely, if ever, been combined in any single person. It had become evident that the force of the Revolution was spent, and that there was a strong recoil in the direction of Monarchy.

Old Sir Jacob Astley's forecast that the various elements of which the Commonwealth party had been composed would quickly become disintegrated after the final defeat of their common enemy, had been amply verified. The Presbyterians, almost to a man, favoured the return of the Stuarts, and the Fifth Monarchy men and other enthusiasts were ready to join any party in overturning the existing order of things.

Under the circumstances it may well be questioned whether, as occupant of the Chair of State during a time of transition, Richard was not an ideal *locum tenens*, and whether his soft and yielding nature and his determination that no blood should be shed in upholding his position, were not the very qualities needed for the situation.

Had Henry succeeded to the Protectorate, it is quite possible that he might have made a successful stand in opposition to the forces arrayed against him, but it would only have been after another cruel and wasteful war, with its legacies of hate and ruin. There is ample evidence to show that the majority of the English people preferred a monarchical form of government, and it is equally certain that at the outset of the quarrel between the King and Parliament, and for long afterwards, there were few indeed who desired to put an end to Monarchy in England. What Cromwell and the other Parliamentary leaders desired was that the Constitution should be changed in accordance with the principles of the Petition of Right passed by the Parliament of 1628. Had Charles then consented, in good faith, to even a moderate limitation of his powers, Cromwell and other Conservative leaders of the popular party would have gladly made terms with him ; but he preferred to be guided by the principles of Laud and Strafford, with which he was in entire sympathy. And so, when Richard descended from the throne, a large section of the more moderate members of the Commonwealth party, wearied of war and general unsettlement, inclined to the hope that the Stuarts, having profited by their heavy experiences, would, if permitted to return, take warning from the errors of Charles and from his terrible fate, and consent to govern the country on more liberal principles. But after being tried again they were finally found wanting, for, like the Bourbons of a later age, they had " learned nothing, and forgotten nothing " in the days of their adversity ; hence, after twenty-eight years of national degradation and most scandalous misgovernment, both in Church and State, almost everything that the Great Protector fought and laboured for had to be for ever secured by the Revolution of 1688.

While Oliver yet remained unburied, and extensive preparations were being made for his funeral, money had to be found for the preliminary expenses. In my collection I have the original order of the New Protector upon his Treasury for £1,500, on that account ; it runs thus :

"Richard, by the grace of God, Lord Protector of the Commonwealth, etc., etc., to the Commissioners of our Treasury and all others the Officers and Ministers of our Exchequer at Westminster to whom these our letters shall appertain and to every of them, Greeting: By the advice of our Privy Councell and for the reasons expressed in their Order of the eight and twentieth day of September in this present year of our Lord, one thousand six hundred and fifty-eight, Our will and pleasure is and we hereby will and command you that out of such our Treasure as is or shall bee remayning in the receipt of our Exchequer by the Customes and Excise or any other branch of our Revenue you forthwith pay or cause to be payd unto John Maidstone, Esquire,* Coferer of our Household the sum of fifteen hundred pounds of lawful money of England to enable him to satisfye and pay for such things as are necessary to be forthwith provided towards the charges of the ffuneral of our most derre Lord and father, Oliver, Lord Protector of blessed memory, and for soe doing this our letter on the inrollment thereof shall bee your sufficient warrant and discharge in this behalfe. Given under our Privie Seale at our Pallace of Westminster the thirtieth day of September, in the yeare of our Lord 1658. Inrolled the 14th day of October, 1658."

The total expenses of the funeral amounted to nearly £30,000, but the £1,500 previously referred to, and a sum of £6,929 6s. 5d. for black cloaks (of which we shall hear again), was all that the country paid towards it, the remainder being left to Richard to pay. Oliver was buried on the 23rd of November following.†

* The writer of the letter to Governor Winthrop of Massachusetts. Thurloe, p. 763. See ante.

† The escutcheon borne at the Protector's funeral is now in the possession of Rev. T. Cromwell Bush, Castle Cary, Somerset, a lineal descendant of Oliver through the Russell marriage.

**Richard Cromwell, born 4th Oct. 1626.** Richard, the third son of the Protector Oliver, was born at Huntingdon, and was educated at Felsted School in Essex ; so as to be under the care of his grandfather, Sir J. Bourchier, who lived there. Nothing is known of Richard's youth, consequently many tales are told of him.

There is reason to believe that he was, nominally, attached to the Army after his father had become Protector, but the profession of arms had evidently no attraction for him, and his accession to power was never popular with the Army in consequence. He chose the law as his profession, and was entered of Lincoln's Inn, 27th May, 1647, but there is no further record of his legal experiences.

On May-day, 1649, after long negotiation on the part of Oliver (as fully set forth in Carlyle), Richard was married to Dorothy Major, of Hursley, in Hampshire. Dorothy's father was a shrewd old man, and when the question of settlements was under discussion, he expressed decided preference for land that had come to Oliver by inheritance, rather than for that obtained by Parliamentary grant from the confiscated estates of Malignant Royalists.

Little is known of Richard's proceedings until he was called to supreme power on the death of his father. He led the life of a country gentleman, apparently taking little note of what was passing in the busy world outside. Evidently his father was not satisfied with his easy going ways, for in a letter to his " Brother Major," Oliver says, " I have committed my son to you, pray give him advice. I would have him mind and understand business, read

HOLOGRAPH LETTER OF "OLIVER P." TO HIS SON RICHARD.

From the original, in the Author's Collection.

a little History, study the Mathematics and Cosmo-
graphy—these are good, with subordination to the
things of God, rather than idleness or mere outward
worldly contentment. These fit for public services
for which a man is born."

Soon after becoming Protector, Richard's troubles
began, and they were mainly caused by those
from whom he had the greatest right to expect un-
stinted service—men like Desborough, Fleetwood,
Lambert, and other great officers of the Army,
who had been raised to place and power by the late
Protector. It had become more and more evident
that the ambition of these men had only been kept
in check by the master spirit to whom they owed
their positions, and great was the delight of the
Royalists in these plottings and exhibitions of dis-
respect towards Richard.

Clarendon, in his *History of the Rebellion*, says :

" The next morning after the death of Oliver, Richard his son
was proclaimed his lawful successor " and was congratulated
by all the authorities, civil and military.  " Foreign princes
addressed their condolences to him and desired to renew
their alliances. . . . so that the King's condition never
appeared so hopeless, so desperate ; for a more favourable
conjuncture his friends could never expect than this, which
now seemed to blast all their hopes, and confirm their utmost
despair."

But what the intrigues of the Royalists failed to
do, was brought about by the enemies of Richard's
own household. Desborough, who had married
Oliver's sister, and Fleetwood, Richard's brother-in-
law, having failed in their objection to Richard's
succession, joined with Lambert and others in

demanding that the appointment of officers in the Army should be taken out of the Protector's hands, on the ground of his being a lawyer ; this was the beginning of his downfall.  Henry Cromwell had no doubt of the disaffection of his relatives in the Army, as he fully showed his brother in a letter from Dublin under date 20th October, 1658—" I thought those whom my father had raised from nothing, would not so soon have forgot him, and endeavoured to destroy his family before he is in his grave . . . Sometimes I think of a Parliament, but am doubtful whether sober men will venture to embark themselves when things are in so high a state of distraction, or, if they would, whether the Army can be restrained from forcing elections. I am almost afraid to come over to your highness, lest I should be kept there and so your highness lose this Army. I also think it dangerous to write freely to you. . . . God help you and bless your Councils." A despairing note, truly !

On the same day Henry Cromwell wrote to his brother-in-law, Fleetwood, entreating him to consider what he was doing before it was too late. " Let me beg you to remember how his late highness loved you ; how he honoured you with the highest trust by leaving the sword in your hand which must defend or destroy us." " Let us remember his last legacy, and, for his sake, render his successor considerable, and not make him vile, a thing of naught, and a by-word."

It soon became evident that the Army was much divided in opinion on public affairs, the Republican party, including most of the superior officers,

Lambert, Fleetwood, etc., desiring to depose the Protector and to re-establish the Commonwealth, while Monk, who commanded in Scotland, had long been an object of suspicion. Richard, therefore, summoned a Parliament, which was duly opened by him on the 27th January, 1658-9. He, or his advisers, thought he would have a more facile assembly if he resorted to the " rotten boroughs " of the Long Parliament, which had been disfranchised by Oliver, but in adopting this course he made a fatal mistake—an act of illegality which was soon followed by another on the part of his enemies in Parliament.

Those old enemies of Oliver—Bradshaw, Scot, Vane, Ludlow and Hazelrig—were members of the new Parliament, and by their eloquence and experience soon obtained the lead of the House, and proceeded to take measures for limiting the power of the Protector and of the " other house." At their sitting of 28th March, 1659, it was resolved, " That it shall be part of this Bill to be brought in, to declare the Parliament to consist of Two Houses," and it was also resolved, " That this House will transact with *the persons* now sitting in the ' other House ' as an House of Parliament during this present Parliament and that it is not hereby intended to exclude such peers as have been faithful to the Parliament from their privileges of being duly summoned to be members of that house." *

The Committee of Army officers continuing their meetings, and rumours of their intentions reaching Parliament, it was resolved at the sitting of 18th April, 1659, "That during the sitting of the Parlia-

* Vide MS. Commons Journal in the Author's collection.

ment there shall be no General Council or meeting of the officers of the Army without the direction, leave or authority, of His Highness the Lord Protector and both Houses of Parliament." *

And it was further resolved that no person should hold any command in the Army or Navy who should refuse to subscribe to an undertaking that he would not disturb the free meetings in Parliament of any of the members of either House, or their freedom in their debates.

**Revolt of the Army Officers, 19th April, 1659.** The passing of these Resolutions becoming known to the Council of Officers, Desborough and Fleetwood were deputed to wait upon the Protector, and to demand a dissolution of Parliament, failing which, they were prepared to put an end to it, in the name of the Army. The officers and others who had remained true to Richard strongly advised him to stand firm and to cause the revolted officers to be arrested and punished, and then to prorogue Parliament. He replied that he "did not love blood," and feeling that the end of his government had come, he complied with the will of those who possessed the power, and signed the act of dissolution on the 22nd April.

**Exit Richard, Protector.** The last time the Protector Richard was referred to in the proceedings of the House of Commons as "His Highness" was on Tuesday, the 19th of April, 1659, upon a motion duly passed, requiring all suspected persons to " depart the Cities of London and Westminster and the lines of communication by the space of twenty miles."†

* Vide MS. Commons Journal in the Author's collection.
† Ibid.

Richard's Protectorate lasted seven months and twenty-eight days.

The supreme authority was now in the hands of Fleetwood and the Council of Officers, and they determined to recall the Rump of the Long Parliament dissolved by Oliver on the 20th April, 1653. Accordingly, on the 7th May, the Speaker of the late Parliament appeared in his place in the House of Commons, and with him many of the old Rump members. He informed them that on the previous day General Lambert had placed in his hands a Declaration in the name of Fleetwood and the Council of Officers, as follows :—
" A declaration of the officers of this army inviting the members of the Long Parliament who continued sitting till the 20th April, 1653, to return to the exercise and discharge of their Trust." At this sitting the members present expressed their purpose to settle the Commonwealth on such a foundation as would secure the prosperity of the people, "and that without a single person, Kingship or House of Peers."

On the 8th May, by resolution of Parliament, Fleetwood was appointed Commander-in-Chief of the armies in England and Scotland, and on the 13th a report from the Committee of Safety was read in the House, recommending that in future the Commander-in-Chief and six officers should nominate all officers of the Army and sign their commissions on behalf of Parliament, which was agreed to.

Tbe Committee of Safety, Mag, 1659. The Committee of Safety, sitting at Wallingford House, had now secured the initiative in all public matters, including the nomination of Judges and dealings

with Foreign Ambassadors. The Mayor of Portsmouth, on the 13th May, notified the Committee
of the fact that 400 Spanish soldiers had been
captured off the Isle of Wight, and that he had
temporarily allowed them fourpence a day for
subsistence. As showing the confusion into which
things had got, the Mayor stated that he had also
communicated the circumstances to the Admiralty,
and had asked for their order, " but not knowing
who now acts in that employment," he thought it his
duty also to tell them.

On the 16th May the House resolved, " That it be
referred  .  .  .  to the Committee of Safety to take
into consideration the present condition of the eldest
son of the late Lord Generall Cromwell, and to
inform themselves what his estate is, and what his
debts are, and how they have been contracted, and
how farre he doth acquiesce in the government of
the Commonwealth as it is declared by this Parliament, and to offer uppon the whole what they
conceive expedient in this behalf, to the Parliament."

At the same sitting it was resolved, " That Whitehall
and Sommersett House be forthwith exposed to sale,
and improved to the best advantage of the Commonwealth, for and towards the sattisfaction and great
arrears due to the Army."

On the 25th May the members appointed to wait
upon Richard Cromwell reported that they had duly
done so, and had obtained his submission to the
present government, along with a statement of his
financial position. The schedule of debts showed
£23,550 to be owing, besides £3,700, which the
"family" had advanced during the past winter for

buying coats for the soldiers, and £609 owing to
Richard for advances to the Dunkirk garrison.

In consideration of Richard's submission, the
Parliament agreed to "putt in oblivion all matters
past as regards the said Richard Cromwell, and to
take upon them his just debts"; at the same time
they requested him to retire from Whitehall, and
instructed the Committee to provide a means for
paying the said debts, and to advance him £2,000
forthwith.

In the meantime, on the 4th July, Sir Arthur
Haselrig moved a resolution in the House which
was adopted, "That the Parliament doth hereby
exempt Richard Cromwell, eldest son of the late
Lord General Cromwell, from all arrests for any
debt whatsoever for six months."

On the 16th July, Parliament ordered that the debt
should be "satisfied by the sale of the plate, hang-
ings, goods and furniture in Whitehall and Hampton
Court, belonging to the State, which may be con-
veniently spared, and that the same be forthwith
sold." Three members of the House were also
instructed to examine as to what goods in the two
palaces were "bought with the State's money," and
to make "a true survey" of the lands and other
property scheduled by Richard.

Nothing further was heard of these just and
generous proposals until the 2nd February, 1659-60,
when it was ordered by Parliament that the money
raised by the sale of the "goods" at Whitehall and
Hampton Court should be applied to the payment of
the Army. So all the fine promises came to naught;
the creditors (presumably) were never paid, and

Richard Cromwell shortly after had to flee to the Continent to avoid arrest on account of them, and to spend twenty years in exile.—" Put not your trust in Princes," nor in Revolutionary Governments.

In my collection of Cromwellian MSS. there is a curious little document, relating to a " shagreen truncke," entirely in the handwriting of Richard Cromwell. Here it is : " Whereas I have formerly delivered to Mrs. Rachell Pengelly my little shagreen truncke which is now in her custody, I doe hereby give and confirme the same and the things there in mentioned unto her the said Rachell Pengelly. But I desire and request her to deliver the said Trunck and the said things contained therein after my death, unto my loving sister Mary Countess ffauconberge upon her payment of the sum of Fifty pounds unto the said Rachell Pengelly, and not otherwise ; and upon such payment I give the said Trunck and the said things it contains unto my said sister to her owne use, witness my hand, this second day of December 1706.

" Richard Cromwell."

One wonders what the trunk contained, and what has become of it. It is related in some of the histories of the time, that when Richard was removing from Whitehall he ordered his servants to be very careful of two old trunks, which stood in his wardrobe. Upon a friend asking him what they contained that he should be so anxious about them, he replied, " Why no less than the lives and fortunes of all the good people of England." They contained the addresses of congratulation upon his accession to power, from all parts of the kingdom.

## CHAPTER XV.

**Provision for Richard Cromwell's "Subsistence."** WHEN the deputation waited upon Richard, by order of Parliament, to ascertain the amount of his debts, they also obtained a statement of his income. This was derived from real estate at Dalby, Newhall, Broughton, Gower, Chopstall, Majore, Wollaston, Chaulton, Burleigh, Oakham, and Egleton, making a total of £7,319 10s. 1d., out of which he had to pay :—

| | | |
|---|---|---|
| To his mother - - - - | £2,000 | os. od. |
| „ „ brother Henry - - | 2,001 | 17s. 9d. |
| „ „ sister Frances - - | 1,200 | os. od. |
| Other annuitants - - - | 818 | os. od. |

Total    £6,019 17s. 9d.

leaving a balance of (say) £1,299 per annum ; but this was encumbered with a debt of £3,000 incurred during his father's lifetime. Before adjourning, on the 25th May, Parliament gave a Committee instructions to consider what was fit to be done to provide a " comfortable and honourable subsistence for the said eldest son of the late Lord Generall Cromwell."

On the 16th July, Parliament received a report from the Committee in which it was recommended that Richard Cromwell's nett income of £1,299 should be made up to £10,000 by Parliament, and that as the annuities payable by him fell in by the death of the recipients, the Parliamentary grant should be reduced accordingly. And it was ordered that this grant should be paid by monthly instalments, the first payment to be made on the "6th day of June next, 1660." No payment was made, nor anything further heard of the "provision for Richard's comfortable and honourable subsistence."

Parliament also undertook to discharge the cost of Oliver's funeral, amounting to nearly £30,000, but there are only records of two amounts having been paid on that account, viz., £1,500 by Richard's order of 30th September, 1658, as already stated, and a sum of £6,929 6s. 5d., paid to "Robert Walton, Citizen and Draper of London for black cloaks by him, sold and delivered for the funeral of the late Lord General Cromwell." On the 2nd February, 1659-60, it was resolved in Parliament that this payment to Walton was an illegal one, and Robert was ordered to refund it !*

The remainder of the Parliamentary proceedings (before the return of the Long Parliament) were of a very kaleidoscopic character, and are of little interest to the present day reader.

**Long Parlia= ment Restored, 22nd Feb., 1659=60.** When Parliament met on the 22nd February, the "excluded" members took their seats once more, and a new Parliament was ordered to assemble on the 25th April, 1660. The House, thus reinforced, passed various votes of a reactionary character,

* Vide MS. Commons Journal, in the Author's collection.

EXECUTION OF THE KING'S JUDGES.

From a rare Dutch engraving, in the Author's Collection.

somewhat to the alarm of Monk, who feared that they would go faster than the Army was prepared to follow. But it became evident that the country had determined to recall the Stuarts ; Charles was proclaimed in various places, and the Common Council of London, in an Address, expressed itself in favour of the Restoration, and they further informed Parliament, " That the City did congratulate the happy return of the Parliament, that they found some persons for a monarchic, some for a Commonwealth, and some *for no Government at all."*

The Restoration  On the 16th March, 1659-60, the
Parliament.  Long Parliament dissolved itself, and the " Restoration " Parliament met on the 25th April ; the King's letters were presented, and he was invited to return, a sum of £65,000 being ordered to be sent him.

Charles made an abundance of promises, including a general amnesty, liberty of conscience, a recognition of all grants, sales and purchases of estates, etc., and only one condition,—which, however, was fatal to every promise,—namely, that his concessions were to be subject to the approval of Parliament. He well knew that Parliament was composed mainly of men whose chief desire was to revenge themselves—for all they had suffered since the beginning of the Civil War—upon their late opponents.

On the 25th May, 1660, King Charles arrived at Dover with the Royal fleet, and was received by General Monk, entering London four days later, on his birthday, and the BLESSED RESTORATION was complete.

There can be no doubt that it was with a sense of relief from overwhelming responsibility that Richard Cromwell descended from the Chair of State. The insane jealousy and ambition of the men around him ; the fanaticism of some and the incompetence of all, clearly enough foreshadowed the ultimate result, and he was willing to let " the potsherds of the earth strive together." The only marvel is that the state of anarchy into which the government of the country was plunged was not sooner taken advantage of by the Royalist party.

And now, Parliament having failed to relieve him from the debts which were only nominally his, Richard found himself in hourly danger of arrest on their account, and being in doubt as to the probable action of the King and his advisers, he determined to leave the country.

Leaving his wife and children at their ancestral home, Hursley Park, near Romsey, Hampshire, he crossed to France,—no attempt being made to detain him ; and for the space of twenty years he wandered about from place to place on the Continent, living under an assumed name, which he changed with every place of abode. Surely there is no more pathetic figure in history than that exhibited in the strange reversal of fortune of this unhappy man. Only a few months before, he had ascended a throne which seemed unassailable by Charles and his courtiers; receiving the congratulations of all the crowned heads of Europe, Louis XIV. being the foremost ; and now he was a wanderer who dared not answer to his name. His wife, to whom he had been married only a few years, and with whom he had been supremely happy, he was destined never to see again, and his youngest daughter, Dorothy, who was born soon after her father became Protector, and was the only Cromwell " born in the purple,"— lived just long enough to receive her father's blessing on her marriage, which she survived but a few months.

Richard Cromwell returned to England in 1680, his wife having been dead five years ; he assumed the name of Clarke, and went to reside with his old friend Mrs. Rachel Pengelly, mother of Serjeant Pengelly, who was then a young law student ; they lived at Cheshunt.

Sir Thomas Pengelly afterwards became Chief Baron of the Exchequer ; his house at Cheshunt was standing till 1880, when it was destroyed by fire ; it must have been a considerable place, as the estimated damage was £10,000.

Richard Cromwell's family consisted of one son, Oliver, and three daughters, Elizabeth, Anne, and Dorothy. When Richard married Dorothy Mayor (or Major) her father settled Hursley upon her husband for life, and by will left it to their son Oliver, subject to his father's life interest. Oliver, by his will, confirmed his father's interest in the estate, and settled it upon trustees, with directions to pay his sisters £2,000 each upon their marriage ; the money to be raised by way of mortgage, or by the sale of timber. Dorothy, dying before Oliver, left her two sisters sole heirs to the property. Anne married a Dr. Gibson in 1698 and was paid her marriage portion ; Elizabeth never married. Oliver died, unmarried, in 1705, only one of his trustees, Benjamin Desboro' (or Disbrowe) a relative of the Cromwell family, surviving him.

Then ensued a prolonged course of unfilial conduct on the part of the two daughters towards their father. Elizabeth, after persuading Disbrowe to renounce his executorship, went up to London with her father to obtain probate of the will as sole executrix ; while there, she managed to give him the slip and went back to Hursley, post haste, and took possession. Richard and Disbrowe vainly tried to get her to give it up, but she resolutely declined to do so, insisting upon her father taking an annuity in lieu of having possession of the estate.

In all this she was encouraged by Dr. Gibson, who had been the cause of much trouble between the brother and sisters. Not content with having ousted Disbrowe from the executorship, Elizabeth tried to remove him from the trusteeship. Failing in her attempts to persuade him to give it up, she moved the Court with that object, alleging that he was " a person in low circumstances." Her real motive was the fact that Disbrowe was a friend of her father's and was determined to protect his interests. She desired to replace Disbrowe with one Gibson, a relative and dependant of her brother-in-law, who would prove himself a willing tool in their hands ; but her efforts were unsuccessful.

In connection with this attempt to prejudice her father's interests, I have an original letter of Benjamin Disbrowe's which, besides being quaint and curious in itself, throws light on the matter ; here it is :—

" *Stifford The* 26 *Sepr*. *1706.*

" *Sr*

" *A man came on purpose from London to leave this supoene att my house, I was not within, but the man tould my wife he had bine downe at Cheshun to serve Richd Cromwell Esqre ye sone of Oliver, but that he theire went by ye name of Mr. Clarke. I hope my Ld Keeper this Terme will either dismiss me, or not tye up my hands, I presume theire is sufficient in ye personall Esteat to have paid Mrs. Spink her interest wch I suppose wd have contented her, it was folly in me, to pt wth executorship I shd have parted with both togither or with none, but it is too late to recall yesterday. After all it will be a great satisfaction to me, if my continuing ye Trust prove servisable to my honored relation, who I think is very much abused. I find there is a great deale of venom in all these vexatious suets, but I hope ye Essew* [issue] *will be to their shame, my hearty service to my honored relation* [R.C.] *att Cheshun, please to accept ye same from Sr yr. humble servant Ben Disbrowe.*

" *If at any time you have any service for me in towne, please to let me knowe it, I shall endeavour to waite upon you. Vale:*

" *For Thos. Pengelly Esqre at his chambers, in Figgtree Court, Inner Temple in London."*

This letter, measuring when folded 3¼ in. × 2¼ in. was sent through the Post Office, and bears the official stamp in a triangle, PENY-POST-PAYD.

Richard, finding remonstrances useless, commenced an action against his daughters for recovery of his rights, Serjeant Pengelly being his Counsel. The principal reason assigned by the daughters and

Gibson for their proceedings, was that Richard, being now old (79) was incapable of managing the estate, and would fritter it away.

In the end judgment was given in Richard's favour, and for the next seven years he resided chiefly at Hursley.

It has been asserted by many persons that Cromwell's daughters did not behave in an unfilial manner to him, the latest apologist for them being Mr. C. Dalton, F.R.G.S., in *Walford's Antiquarian.* He bases his contention (1) upon there being no documentary evidence in support of the charge, and (2) on the fact that Richard had written a very affectionate letter to his daughter Anne. But this letter was written in 1690—fifteen years before the death of Oliver, and when there were no questions in dispute respecting the property; moreover, it was before the disturbing element of the Gibson marriage embittered matters. Unfortunately, Mr. Walton is equally in error as to the absence of documentary evidence. I happen to have in my possession all the original documents in the case—including the affidavits of all the parties, Counsel's speeches, and the Judge's decision. The Decree was made in December, 1706, and was entirely in Richard's favour, the only condition being that he was to account to a Master in Chancery for all monies received. It does not appear that any of the parties appeared in Court, the evidence being by affidavit. They would most likely come before a Master in Chambers.

After the trial the father became reconciled to his children, dividing his time between his friends at Cheshunt and his daughter Elizabeth at Hursley. On

Sunday mornings he attended the parish church with her, going in the afternoon to a Baptist chapel in Romsey, riding in his coach alone.

Very little is known of the ex-Protector's doings during his twenty years exile, but it is known that in 1666 his name was included, with others, in a Proclamation requiring their presence in England to answer certain charges. Mrs. Cromwell, in a state of great anxiety, sent her servant, W. Mumford, to London to obtain exact information, but ultimately his name was withdrawn.

In connection with the Proclamation, Cromwell's servant was examined on behalf of the Crown as to what he knew of his master's doings. He declared he had been in the service of the family for eleven years, and that he had spent the previous year (1665) with him in Paris, where he was known as John Clark. He (Cromwell) saw no visitors except certain Frenchmen who instructed him in the Sciences. " His whole diversion was drawing of landscapes and reading of books." He further stated that the estate of Richard Cromwell, in right of his wife, was but £600 a year, and that " he knoweth Richard Cromwell is not sixpence the richer or better off for being the son of his father, or for being the pretended Protector of England." He further stated that the estate of old Mrs. Cromwell (Oliver's widow), lately deceased, was in the hands and management of Jeremy White, chaplain to Oliver, " now living with Sir John Russell at Chippenham, who will not come to any account for the same." Fie ! old Jeremiah, of whom we hear no more. Mumford's statement was accepted, and Richard Cromwell was not troubled.

Richard Cromwell died 12th July, 1712, at the house of his old friends the Pengelly's at Cheshunt, and was buried in the chancel of Hursley Church. He enjoyed good health to the last, and at the age of eighty could gallop his horse for several miles. He is described as having been tall, fair-haired, and "the lively image of his father." Certainly there is a great resemblance in their portraits, although Richard's countenance lacks the sternness and majesty of his father's, and he had no " wart."

John Howe, the chaplain to both Oliver and Richard, had a high respect for the latter, and Dr. Isaac Watts, who, as a young man, was often in Richard's company, testified to his abilities as being by no means contemptible. Unprejudiced authorities all concur in describing him as having been a humane man, kind-hearted, and sagacious. Shortly before his death he said to his two attendant daughters,

"Live in love ;
I am going to the God of Love."

I have in my possession a remarkable collection of letters, statements of expenditure, law papers, etc., dealing with the ex-Protector's life, from 1680, when he returned to England, to 1712, when he died. The accounts were kept by Cromwell's old friend, Mrs. Rachel Pengelly, and are in great detail. From them we learn that the whilom occupant of the Throne of England, Lord Protector of Great Britain and Ireland, master of the palaces of Whitehall and Hampton Court, and for whom Parliament voted £10,000 a year, as "provision for his comfortable and honourable subsistence," lived in lodgings at Cheshunt for several years before his death, paying ten shillings a week for his board, and having due allowance made for his occasional periods of absence. But there were evidently "extras" to this charge, for we find Mrs. Pengelly, in her monthly bills, charging four and sixpence for "the Sturgeon you ordered Nan to bye"; and on another occasion "one ginney" is charged for "sammon, oysters, and wild fowl."

At the same time, two shillings are "down" for "black cherry beare," as drink for the table. But Richard liked an occasional taste of some more potent beverage, for I find frequent entries of payments for brandy. He also indulged in the Virginia weed, spending considerable sums for tobacco;—but then his "pypes" were very inexpensive—two shillings and eightpence per gross! On one occasion the ex-Protector borrows £2 from his landlady, "when you had your feast." After this one is not surprised at finding an item of payment for some bottles of "surfeit water." There are several entries for "pype-burning, and ishue paper,"—did he "colour" his pipes, like the youth of the present day? Occasionally, Richard's daughters would come up from Hursley, and then he would treat them to dinner at Westminster; but before leaving his lodgings he would require money, and Mrs. Pengelly enters in her account, "When you dined with the Ladyes, 20 shillings." If the ladies dined with their father at his lodgings we find, "When the ladyes dined here, fowls 5s." and for afternoon refreshment, "A quarter pound of Tee, five shillings, and

Shuger lofe for Tee, four and sixpence." And when
" Mr. Clark," or "the gentilman " (by which names
Mr. Cromwell was known) had fowls for his dinner,
Mrs. Pengelly debits him with eighteenpence for
" Backon and suit " for " stuffing."

Here is an item for " Phissick drink": "Yerbs, six
lemmons, and bushell of malt to brew the drink, five
shillings." Mrs. Pengelly is also careful in her
attention to her lodger's wardrobe ; she pays " half
a ginney for Callichoe Wascots and makeing"; " for
mending and lacquering your shoes, eighteen pence,"
and "for repairing your breeches, sixpence." "For
a pair of striped breeches, thirty-four shillings," and
here is an item that Oliver never indulged in, viz.,
" Perriwigs," for which we find Richard paying a
guinea each (guineas were reckoned at thirty shillings
each in 1695). An Irish "frees" coat cost twenty-five
shillings, and a new " hatt," thirty shillings, and
" muslin Cravats " two shillings each.

Incidentally we find that Cromwell wore " muffs "
and that he used spectacles, for there is an entry for
one shilling for " case for your spectacals "; but it
does not appear that at that time " Mr. Clark" paid
much attention to literature, the only payment for
books being one shilling for an "Almanack" for
1693. The only dissipation with which Richard
is credited—or rather debited—in Rachel Pengelly's
account is when she advanced him " ten shillings on
Lord Mayor's day when you dined with Mr.
Disbrowe." Richard, late " Chief of the State," had
now to pay tribute to Cæsar—Dutch William—as is
evidenced by this entry in Mrs. Pengelly's account
in 1689 : "Paid ye King's Pole [tax] for you,

a gentleman, one ginney;" subsequent entries for this tax were only eleven shillings.

That he was kind to children, and to young people generally, is clear, there being numerous entries of payments for presents for them ; to Mrs. Aldersey's child he gives "muffs and ribbons," also a "whisell and corralls with ribbons," costing more than six pounds. To "Goody Odle's child he gives gloves and a fan."

To young Thomas Pengelly, who afterwards successfully conducted his law suit, Richard is very kind, Mrs. Pengelly gratefully acknowledging, "Money you were pleased to give Tommy on his entrance at the Temple £3 18s. od.," and a guinea towards buying his law books. But "Tommy" must have a gun, so his kind friend gives him fifteen shillings wherewith to buy one ; let us hope it was not more dangerous to him than to the "wild fowl" so dear to "Mr. Clark." Mrs. Pengelly writes to her son "Tommy" that she has sent him a basket of "Progg," which she hopes will prove "toothsome."

In the year in which Charles II. died (1685) Cromwell presented his daughter Anne with a new "Tippitt," and to her sister, Madam Betty, a box of gloves ; but he does not appear to have gone into mourning for the King. Ten years later, when Queen Mary died, Mrs. Pengelly records that Richard expended half-a-crown upon "mourning gloves" in honour of that monarch's memory.

Occasionally Richard would spend a few weeks with his daughters at Hursley, and in one of his letters to Mrs. Pengelly he explains a postponement of his return by giving her "the forcible argument of the want of a shirt. Madam Betty went to buy one, but instead of buying, she borrowed, so that I shall have to have mine washed which I hope to bring upon my back to Cheshunt shortly"; and he adds, "there is a matter of business that cannot speak by a *penny post* letter."

Between Richard Cromwell and his sister Mary, Countess of Fauconberg,* there existed a life-long affection ; frequent references are made to her in his letters to Mrs. Pengelly, and he gives an account of a visit he made at her "new town house" in 1709, but in none of his correspondence, nor in that of his friends, is there any reference to his former condition.

There are now no descendants of Oliver Cromwell in the male line, but they continue to flourish in the following families, amongst others : The Marquis of Ripon, the Villiers family, Earls of Clarendon, the Vyners of Kingston Hill, Surrey, Sir John Lubbock, M.P., Sir William Harcourt, and Dr. Samuel Rawson Gardiner, author of the standard works on Cromwell and the Commonwealth Period.

THE END.

* Lady Fauconberg survived her brother one year, dying in 1713, leaving no family.

# ADDENDA.

---

## THE PORTRAITS OF OLIVER CROMWELL.

"Stands some 5ft. 10in.—or more ; a man of strong, solid stature, and dignified—now, partly military carriage ;—the expression of him valour and devout intelligence, energy, and delicacy on a basis of simplicity. Fifty-four years old, gone April last, brown hair and moustache are getting grey. A figure of sufficient impressiveness—not lovely to the man-milliner species, nor pretending to be so. Massive stature, big, massive head, of somewhat leonine aspect; wart above the right eyebrow; nose of considerable blunt-aquiline pro-portions; strict, yet copious lips, full of all tremulous sensi-bilities, and also, if need were, of all fierceness and rigors; deep, loving eyes, call them grave, call them stern, looking from under those craggy brows as if in lifelong sorrow, and yet, not thinking it sorrow, thinking it only labour and endeavour; on the whole, a right noble lion-face, and hero-face, and, to me, royal enough."—*Carlyle.*

### OLIVER, COMMANDER-IN-CHIEF.

Portrait, with Staff of Office, and with his page adjusting his scarf. This portrait formerly belonged to Earl Spencer, and is now in the National Portrait Gallery. It is a beautiful specimen of Walker's painting.

### PORTRAIT OF OLIVER (ENGRAVED).

Under one of these is this quaint inscription :
> " Made Nations bow
> And preached down mitral evils,
> Parsons outpray'd
> And vanquished prophane devils."

## PORTRAIT OF OLIVER, LORD PROTECTOR.
### By Walker.

In the possession of Rev. T. Cromwell Bush, Rector of Duloe, Cornwall.

(Mr. Bush possesses Walker's receipt.)

## PORTRAIT OF OLIVER. (†)

Half-length, in armour—believed to be an original. It was found in a loft at the former residence of one of Cromwell's Major Generals.

Pistol shots had been - fired through the eye and other parts.

## MINIATURE OF OLIVER. (†)

Half-length, in armour, by Van Berg, a Dutch Artist (signed and dated).

## PORTRAIT OF OLIVER BY LELY.

This portrait was painted by Sir Peter Lely in 1653. Better than any other it illustrates the rugged grandeur and majesty of Oliver's countenance. While engaged in his task, the painter hesitatingly asked the Protector if he should show the wart over his right eye ? Said Oliver : " You will paint me exactly as I am, with all my warts, humours, and blemishes."

The picture was presented by Oliver to the Grand Duke of Tuscany, and is now in the Pitti Palace at Florence.

I have an excellent copy in my Collection. Oliver had had a little State transaction with the Grand Duke, which had raised the Protector in his estimation mightily.

Certain English merchants had been robbed of property to the value of £40,000 by the Duke or his officers, and he had contemptuously refused to make amends. No English ships of war had been seen in the Mediterranean since the Crusades, and English ships had been at the mercy of Algerian pirates and piratical Grand Dukes, so Oliver despatched Admiral Blake with thirty-five ships to bring the pirates to reason. This he quickly did ; the Grand Duke paid the £40,000, and craved the honour of the Great Protector's portrait. After its arrival, the Duke sent a splendid ebony cabinet of perfumes to Oliver, which is now in the possession of Rev. T. Cromwell Bush, of Duloe, Cornwall.

"OLIVER BETWEEN THE PILLARS."

From the celebrated print by W. Faithorne.

## DUTCH PORTRAITS OF OLIVER.

These are for the most part semi-caricatures. There is one signed " IOOST HARTGERS EXENDIT " and entitled " OLIVIER CROMWEL Luÿtenant-Generael van de Armee van 't Parlement van Engelandt," which makes Oliver appear to have a wooden head. Perhaps it was the work of a wood engraver! Any way, the Dutch Statesmen, with their Admirals De Ruyter and Van Tromp, did not think the Protector had a wooden head! (See page 118.)

## FAITHORNE'S CELEBRATED ENGRAVING OF "OLIVER BETWEEN THE PILLARS."

The inscription at foot of the picture says :—

" The emblem of England's destructions, also of her attained and further expected Freedom and happiness." Oliver is represented standing between two columns ; under his right foot is a discrowned King, and under his left a dragon, representing Faction and Error. The column on his right is surmounted by Oliver's favourite device of the Sun and Moon, O C, and on the shaft of the Column are inscriptions, such as

Constantia Fortitudo,
Lex Corona Columna,
Salus Populi Suprema Lex, and
Magna Charta.

The Column on the Protector's left is surmounted by a view of Westminster Hall, from the door of which issues a riband with the device, " Bee still and know that I am God." In his right hand he holds the Sword of State, having the crowns of the three kingdoms on it, while from its point another riband is unfolded, having the motto, " I will never leave thee, nor forsake thee." On the top left hand corner is a picture showing the Ark resting on Ararat, and below it Abraham offering up Isaac. On the right hand the Ark is also seen between Scylla and Charybdis, but how it got there is not explained.

At the bottom right hand corner the Devil is busy with a pickaxe, a gallows being handy at his side. A man is seen fanning a fire with a pair of bellows, while others are ploughing, tending sheep, etc., the motto below being, " They shall beat their spears into pruning hooks, and their swords into plow-shares."

In a later impression the head of William III. has been substituted for that of Cromwell. A copy in this state is in the Pepysian Collection at Magdalen College.

## GEORGE III. AND OLIVER CROMWELL.

In my collection is one of Gillray's caricature repre-
sentations of our bovine monarch, holding a Cooper miniature
in one hand and a candle in the other. The expression on
the King's face is one of speechless horror. Caricaturists
seem to have had considerable license when Gillray produced
this picture (18th June, 1792), for it is a gross representation
of the royal features. The principal portion of George's head
is the part containing the mouth, in a line drawn from the
lower part of the ear to the upper portion of the eye.

Certainly, from an intellectual point of view, George III.
was unfit to hold a candle to the uncrowned King.

———

There is only one statue of the Great Protector in all England! * A civil engineer—all honour to him—offered to present
one to the town of Leeds about the year 1870, but it was declined
on the ground that public opinion was not ripe for such an
innovation! ‡ In 1860 several Manchester gentlemen subscribed £100 each towards a statue, T. B. Potter, M.P., and
Alderman Goadsby being amongst the number, but the cotton
famine coming on at the time, the project was abandoned.
In 1875, however, the widow of Mr. Goadsby, who had then
become the wife of Alderman Heywood, carried out Mr.
Goadsby's intention, and the fine statue by Noble was erected
on the very spot where the first man killed in the Parliamentary War is said to have fallen. The statue stands on a
pedestal of rough hewn granite, and bears the inscription,
"Oliver Cromwell," with the dates of his birth and death,
and the words, "The gift of Elizabeth Salisbury Heywood to
the citizens of Manchester, 1875."

## IVORY TANKARD (Artist Unknown). (†)

This carving is a reproduction of West's famous picture.

The tankard is very finely carved, is 18 inches in height,
and 8 inches in diameter at the base. The cover is surmounted
by the figure of a Roman senator in his toga.

The moment chosen by the artist is when Oliver, stepping
forward, orders his men to "Take away that bauble." The

---

* Thanks to the patriotic munificence of a distinguished nobleman, this reproach
will now cease to exist. Mr. Thornycroft has completed a splendid bronze statue
of the Protector, which will be on view at the Royal Academy on May 1st, and
afterwards be erected near the Houses of Parliament.

‡ *The Pictorial World*, 18th December, 1875.

RICHARD P.
From the original, in the Author's Collection.

Speaker in his chair is horrified at the profanation of the Chamber by the Military, and, on his right, Sir Henry Vane stretches out his hands in protest against the General's high-handed proceeding.

## THE DEATH MASK. (†)

Bears unmistakable evidences of its being genuine. The large face and large features, the wart over the right eyebrow, and the general appearance, are all strikingly like the portraits, especially that painted by Lely. It is known that Oliver usually wore his moustache, and a tuft under his lower lip ; it is also known that during his daughter's illness he refused to be shaved, and the mask shows a fortnight's growth. ↘

## RICHARD CROMWELL, PROTECTOR. (†)

Presentation of a Minister to the Living of Buckland, in Gloucestershire.

Richard, P.

Richard Lord Protector of the Commonwealth of England, Scotland, and Ireland, and the Dominions and Territories thereunto belonging to the Commissioners authorised by the Ordinance for Approbation of Publique Preachers under date 20th Mch., 1654, consisting of 38 members, Fras. Rouse, Provost of Eton, being at their head or any five of them Greeting We present Mr. Samuel Gardner to the Rectory of Buckland in our County of Gloucester voyd by the relinquishment of Mr. Joseph Cobb, the last Incumbent there and to our presentation belonging to the end he may be approved of by them and admitted thereunto with all its rights, members, and appurtenances whatsoever, according to the tenor of the aforesaid ordinance given at White Hall the eleaventh day of January, in the year of our Lord one thousand six hundred and fifty-eight.

(Seal)

## OLIVER  P. (†)

A similar document, signed "OLIVER P.," nominating "Mr. Frauncis Gibson" to the Rectory of Miningsby in Lincolnshire.

## CROMWELL AND THE JEWS.

The Jews had been excluded from England for centuries, but in the 17th century they tried to return, and knowing the straits to which Charles I. was reduced by lack of money, they sent an embassy to him and offered £500,000 for the town of Brentford, if they might be allowed to settle in England once again. Charles would no doubt have accepted the offer, but his Ministers foresaw a storm if they were permitted to return, as the trading classes and clergy were well known to be strongly opposed to it.

Under the Protectorate the attempt was renewed; a deputation came over from Amsterdam, headed by the learned Rabbi, Manasseh Ben Israel, with the object, first, of obtaining permission to build a synagogue in London, for which privilege they offered the Protector the sum of £60,000, and secondly, for leave once again to settle in the country. Oliver was quite prepared to assent to the request, and summoned a meeting of the clergy and chief merchants of London to hear the Rabbi in public audience, and to discuss the question. The meeting was held in the Long Gallery at Whitehall. Having called upon the Rabbi to state his case, the Protector turned to the clergy, asking their opinion, upon which they strongly inveighed against the Jews, calling them "a cruel and accursed people."

In vain did Oliver ask the clergy if it were not their duty to preach the Gospel to all, remarking that he proposed to make that easy for them, in the case of the Jews, by bringing them to England. They were silenced but not convinced. He then turned to the merchants, who spoke much of the falseness and meanness of the Jews, and said that, if admitted into England, they would get all the trade of the country into their hands.

Oliver thereupon began to abuse the Jews, and after saying everything that was contemptuous about them, went on: "Can you really be afraid that this mean, despised people should be able to prevail in trade and credit over the merchants of England, the noblest and most esteemed merchants of the whole world?" The merchants, too, were silenced, but not convinced, and when Oliver, as a Constitutional Ruler, laid the matter before Parliament, his wishes were overruled. Nevertheless, as the Executive authority, he did not put the exclusion laws into operation, allowing them to lapse, and so the Jews came back to

England. Oliver also allowed Manasseh Ben Israel a pension of £100 a year.

Two and half centuries after the interview above described, a Jewish gentleman in London, Mr. Charles Wertheimer, remembering how Cromwell had befriended the Jewish race, purchased Bernini's magnificent bust of the Protector from Lord Revelstoke's collection at a cost of £1,400, and presented it to the Nation, and it now stands in the House of Commons corridor.

The Bust is the work of the celebrated Sculptor, Painter and Architect, BERNINI.

b. 1598-d. 1680.

The acceptance of this Bust by Parliament makes some amends for the refusal of the last Parliament—at the churlish instance of the Irish members—to accept a Statue on behalf of the Nation.

## CROMWELL AND THE QUAKERS.

On three occasions the Protector gave audience to George Fox, and there seemed to be much in common between them. At their first interview, George Fox discoursed on the doctrines of the new sect, Oliver appearing to be much interested, and on some gentlemen coming into the room, the Protector took George Fox's hand, and with moistened eyes, said, "Come again to my house; if thou and I were but an hour of the day together, we should be nearer the one to the other. I wish no more harm to thee than I do to my own soul." And so they parted for that time.

The last time the Quaker and the Protector met was a few days before Oliver's death.

George Fox thus tells the story: "Taking boat, I went to Kingston, and from thence to Hampton Court, to speak with the Protector about the sufferings of Friends; I met him riding into Hampton Court Park; and before I came to him, as he rode at the head of his Life Guard, I saw and felt a waft of death go forth against him; and when I came to him, he looked like a dead man. After I had laid the sufferings of Friends before him . . . he bade me come to his house.

"So I returned to Kingston, and the next day went up to Hampton Court to speak further with him. But when I came, Harvey, who was one that waited on him, told me that the doctors were not willing that I should speak with him. So I passed away and never saw him more."

There is an amusing reference to Cromwell in the *Life of John Roberts*, a contemporary Quaker. On his (Roberts) appearing in an ecclesiastical Court on some trumpery charge, the Bishop asked him how many children he had? "I have had seven," said John, "of whom it hath pleased the Lord to remove three by death."—"And have they all been bishoped?" [*i.e.*, confirmed]—"No," said the witty Quaker, "for most of them were born in Oliver's time, when Bishops were out of fashion." "At which," says the old chronicler, "the Court fell a-laughing."

There can be no doubt that Cromwell was very well-disposed towards the Quakers, for he showed it in various ways, notably in his protest against the cruel punishment inflicted by the Presbyterian Parliament upon the poor, mad enthusiast, James Naylor.

George Fox evidently thought that being the head of the Government, Oliver had but to say the word and all persecution would cease, and that as he did *not* say the word, he was responsible. And there are some people at the present day who think that because the Czar of Russia is an Autocrat, he is responsible for the persecution of the Stundists and other Dissenters in that country.

## REV. JEREMIAH WHITE, FRANCES CROMWELL AND THE WAITING-MAID.

It is said of Oliver Cromwell, that he had the most perfect system of espionage, by which he was able to circumvent the numberless Royalist and other plots that were continually being hatched against his Government.

But, although filled with the cares of State, he was not unmindful of his family and all that concerned their welfare. Overwhelmed with public affairs, marching and fighting, negotiating with the King and contending with a reactionary Parliament, he yet found time to arrange the marriage of his eldest son, Richard, to the daughter of a Hampshire squire. Nor did he forget his daughters: Elizabeth, his favourite, was married to Claypole, his Master of the Horse, Bridget became the wife of Major Ireton, and Frances married the Hon. Mr. Rich, heir to the Earl of Warwick. But Mr. Rich was not the first suitor for the hand of Frances. Word was one day brought to Oliver that his trusted Chaplain, the Rev. Jeremiah White, was indulging in fond hopes of winning the favour of the Lady Frances.

On hearing this he caused a watch to be set upon the doings
of the ambitious priest, who was shortly discovered in the
lady's boudoir. Oliver at once repaired there, and found the
reverend Jeremiah on his knees before his daughter. In
menacing tones he demanded what he did there. "An't
please your Highness," said the wary and terrified priest, "I
was only soliciting her ladyship's permission to marry her
waiting-woman." A grim smile passed over the features of
the Protector, who replied, "Then I will see that your prayer
is granted, for you shall be married before you leave this
room!"

Calling the lady's maid, Oliver told her what an honour the
rev. gentleman proposed to do her, ending by saying that
he would himself provide her dowry. The young woman was
delighted, and they were forthwith married, Dr. Godwin per-
forming the ceremony.

Copy of letter (†) from Sir Francis Russell, kinsman of
Cromwell's, to Rev. Jeremiah White (candidate for the hand
of the Protector's daughter):

"Sir,

"I spake unto Jack to let you understand why I sent you
not this by him, because indeed it deserves you shd know how
great a benefit I doe still receive by that advise I had from
you as to my infirmity of the strangury, and truly I hope it
may so continue still with me, if so be I can but take a care
of my dyeat, and bewar of catching cold. I must needs
confesse I did once despaire of ever enjoying so much health
as I have done of late, I meane since I tryed yr experyment,
yet upon any remarkable change of weather I am put in mind
that the root of my disease doeth still ly hid within me : but
I hope it will be of good use and a right instruction to my
mind and spirit, because some kind of rod or other is needful
for us all while we are but young, or children, for few or none
will learne obedience or wisedome without it, and among the
weake and ignorant I am one of the chiefest. Pray Sr let me
at yr leisure understand how it is with Will : Sedgewick, and
what becomes of Dick Norton's crop of wheat. I have no
country news for you, onely that my Lord of St. Albons is come
into these parts where he was nobly and kindly received by
his neighbours and countrymen. You have obliged me to
be Sr.

"Your true friend to serve you
"Franc : Russell.
"Chip. Sep. 20th, 1663."

Sealed with crest and addressed :
  " For his very loving friend
        Mr. Jeremiah White
  Leave this att the black Bell in St. Paul's Churchyard,
London,"
  Sir F. Russell was the father-in-law of Henry Cromwell who
lived with him, or near him, after the Restoration.

## THE FORME OF THE WRITT OF SUM̄ONS.

Oliver Lord Protector of the Com̄onwealth of England
Scotland and Ireland and the Dominions & territoryes thereunto belonging To our trusty and wel beloved sonne Lord
Richard Cromwell Greeting whereas by the advise and
assent of Our Councell for certaine great and weighty
affaires concerning US, the State and defence of the said
Com̄onwealth We ordained Our prsent Parliamt to be held
at Our City of Westmr, the 17th day of September,
in the yeare of Our Lord one thousand six hundred ffifty and
six & there to consult and aduise wth the knights Citizens
and burgesses of Our said Commonwealth, wch Parliamt was
then & there held and Continued vntil the six and
twentieth day of June last past and then adjourned vntill the
XXth day of January now next Coming. Therefore we com̄-
and and firmely enioyne you that Considering the difficulty
of the said affaires and eminent Dange y all excuses being
set aside you be psonally present at Westmr afore said the
said twentieth day of January next Coming, there to treat
conferre and giue yor advise with VS and with the Great
men and Nobles in and concerning the affaires aforesaid, and
this as you loue or honor and safety and the defence of
the Com̄onwealth aforesaid you shall in no wise omitt witnes
or selfe at Westmr the nineth day of december in the
yeare of Our Lord one thousand six hundred ffifty and seven.
  The like writts were directed to the severall persons
following vizt,
Lord Henry Cromwell Deputy of Ireland
Nathaniel Fiennes one of the Lordes Com̄rs of the Great Seale
John Lisle one of the Lordes Com̄rs of the Great Seale
Henry Laurence Presidt of ye Priuy Councell
Charles Fleetwood Leut Genll of ye Army
Robert Earle of Warwick
Edward Earle of Manchester
Edmond Earle of Mulgrave

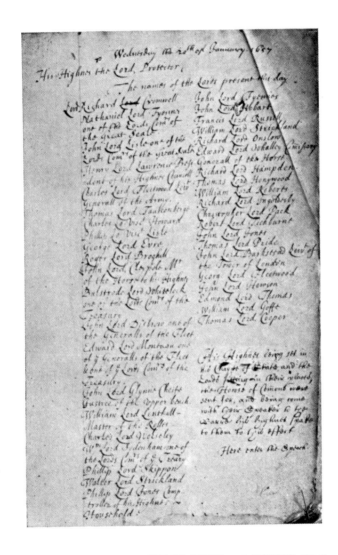

THE OPENING OF PARLIAMENT BY OLIVER, 20TH JANUARY, 1657-58.
From the original MS. in the Author's Collection (Journal of the House of Lords).

David Earle of Cassils
Wm Lord Visc^t Say & Seale
Tho : Lord Falconberge
Charles Lord Visc^t Howard
Phillip Lo. Visc^t Lisle
S^r Gilbert Pickering barronet Chamblen of his Highnes
 houshold
George Lord Evers
Phillip Lord Wharton
Roger Lord Broghill
William Pierreponte esq^r
John Lo. Cleypole M^r of the Horse to his Highness
S^r Bulstrode Whitelock one of y^e Lordes Com^rs of y^e
 Treary
John Disbrow one of y^e Gen^lles of the Fleet
Edward Montagu one of y^e Generalles of y^e Fleet & one of
 the Lordes Com^rs of y^e Treary
George Monck Comaunder in cheife of y^e forces in Scotland
John Glynne cheife Justice assigned to hold pleas before his
 Highness in the Vpper bench
Wm Lenthall M^r of y^e Rolls in Chauncery
Oliver S^t John cheife Justice of y^e Court of Comon pleas
Wm Steele Chancellor of Ireland
S^r Charles Wolseley barronet
W^m Sidenham one of y^e Lordes Com^rs of the Treary
Phillip Skippon esq^r
Walter Strickland esq^r
Francis Rous esq^r
Phillip Jones esq^r Comptroller of his Highnes Houshold
John Fiennes esq^r
S^r John Hobart barr^t
S^r Gilbt Gerrard barr^t
S^r Arthur Heselrigge bar^t
S^r Francis Russel bar^t
Sr W^m Strickland K^t & bar^t
S^r Rich. Onslow K^t
Edward Whalley Com^ry Gen^ll of y^e horse
Alexander Popham esq^r
John Crew esq^r
S^r W^m Lockart Kt          Rich Hampden esq^r
S^r Tho. Honiwood k^t        S^r W^m Roberts kt
S^r Archibald Johnsson of Warreston
Rich. Ingoldsby esq^r
S^r Chr. Pack kt

S$^r$  Ro. Tichburne
S$^r$  Tho. Pride kt
John Jones esq$^r$
S$^r$ John Barkstead kt Lew$^t$ of the Tower of London
S$^r$  Geo Fleetwood
S $^r$ Mathew Tomlinson kt
S$^r$  John Hewson kt
Edmond Thomas, esq$^r$
James Berry esq$^r$
Wm Goffe esq$^r$
Thomas [Cooper esq$^r$ —torn off]
The names of such Lordes as have delivered in their writts of
      Sumõns to this present Parliam$^t$.   Insert y$^e$ names
      of the persones Sworne.

---

    The Parliament begun and held at Westm$^r$ the 17th day
of September, 1657, being adjourned by Act of Parliam$^t$
vntill this present XXth day of January, 1657-58.  His
Highness the Lord Protector having according to the
Humble addiconall and explanatory peticon and Advice,
caused writts of Sumõns to be ysshued to diverse hono$^{ble}$
persons to sitt in this House, retornable this day, about nine
of the Clock in the morning there came into the Little roome
within the painted Chamber, The Lord Comĩssioner Fyennes
and the Lord Comĩr Lisle, Lords Comĩssione$^{rs}$ of the Great
Seale, the Lord President of his Highnes Councell,
Gen$^{ll}$ John Disbrowe, Phillip Jones, esq$^r$ Comptroller of his
Highnes Household, and S$^r$ Bulstrode Whitelock, K$^t$, Con-
stable of the Castle of Windsor and one of the Lords Comĩrs
of his Highnes Treasury vnto whom (w$^{th}$ others) a Comĩssion
vnder the Great Seale was directed authorizing them or any
three or more of them to administer to the persons called to
sitt in this house, the Oath directed by the said humble
addiconall and explanatory peticon and Advice, w$^{ch}$ Comĩssion
being read by the Clerke of the Comõnwealth in Chauncery,
the said Oath was first taken by the Lord Comĩssioner
ffyennes, the Lord Com$^r$ Lisle, and the Lord president of his
highnes Councell, and then administered by them vnto the
rest of the Comĩssioners present and afterwards was taken
in their presence by—
The Lord Richard Cromwell
Charles Fleetwood, Leiv$^t$ Generall of the Army
The Lord Faulconberge
Charles Lo. Visc$^t$ Howard

Phillip Lo. Visc^t Lisle

George Lord Evre

Roger Lord Broghill

John Lord Cleypole M^r of the Horse to his Highnes

Edward Montagu One of the Generalls of y^e Fleet & one of
the Lords Comission^rs of the Treasury

John Glynne Cheife Justice assigned to hold pleas before his
Highnes in y^e upper Bench

W^m Lenthall M^r of y^e Rolles

S^r Charles Wolseley bar^t

W^m Sydenham one of y^e Lords Com^rs of y^e Treary

Phillip Skippon esqr

Walter Strickland esq^r

John Fiennes esqr

S^r John Hobart Bar^t

S^r Fran: Russell bar^t

S^r W^m Strickland k^t & bar^t

S^r Rich Onslow kt

Edward Whalley Com^ry of the Horse

Richard Hampden esqr

S^r Tho. Honywood kt

S^r W^m Roberts kt

Rich. Ingoldsby esq^r

S^r Chr. Pack kt

S^r Robt Tichburne kt

John Jones esq^r

S^r Thomas Pride kt

Sr John Barkstead k^t Leiv^t of y^e Tower of London

S^r John Geo Fleetwood kt

S^r John Hewson kt

Edmond Thomas esqr

William Goffe esqr

Thomas Cooper esqr

    The Tenor of the Comission for administring the oath
aforesaid was as followeth

[Not filled in.]

---

25th  MAY, 1655.

By the Com^ee for the Admiralty & Navy.

    In pursuance of an order of the Councell dated the 13th of
Aprill 1655, whereby it is referred to the said Com^ee to take

order that Cloth and bayes be provided for Coatts for his
Highnes watermen & to transmitt to the Councell a Note of
the price thereof; The said Com^ee doe humbly transmitt the
Note annexed as the price of the said Coates, amounting to
the sume of Thirty nine pounds One shilling, and Six pence
desireing order may be given for payment of the same
accordingly.

And Colonell Jones is desired to report
ye same.

Ex Ro: Blackborne Secr^s :

for Watermens Coats

Delivered by order of the Right
Hon^ble the Com^ee for the Ad^ty : & Navy
Ap^ll 27th.

In y^e 39 yds of Red Cloth Lond^n measure att 13s 6d

|   | £ | s | d |
|---|---|---|---|
| - - - - - - - | 26 | 06 | 06 |
| It 78 yds of Red bayes att 2^s 6^d | 09 | 15 | 00 |
| It. 4 yds of Red Cloth for Mr Nutt Master of his Highnesse Barges att 15^s - - - - | 03 | 00 | 00 |
|   | 39 | 01 | 06 |

by me

ROBERT   WANTON.


## OLIVER, AS CHIEF CONSTABLE AND GAME PRESERVER! (†)

### OLIVER P.

By his Highness the Lord Protector.

These are to authorize and impower S^r William Paston
Barr^t. his sufficient Deputy & Deputies or either of them
to seize & take away all Gunns. Tranells, Netts, Snares,
or other unlawfull Engines from any Person or Persons
within Seaven Myles of Oxnitt, in the County of Norfolke,
who shall use or keepe the same contrary to the Law.
And also to seize & take away all Greyhoundes Setting-
doggs, or Spannells from any Person or Persons who shall
use them in taking or destroying of Phesants, Herons,
Ducks & Mallards Partridges or Hares w^thin Seaven Myles
of Oxnitt aforesaid contrary to y^e Lawes and Statutes of

this Comon-Wealth. These are also to authorize the said Sr William Paston, and his sufficient Deputy and Deputies or either of them to apprhend the Parties soe offending & carry them to the next Justice of Peace within the said County to be punished according to their demeritts. These are further to require all High-Constables, Constables and all other Officers to be aydeing and assisting to the said Sr William Paston and his Deputy and Deputies in the due Execucon of this Warrant Given att White-Hall the fourteenth of June 1656.

seal.

(endorsed)
> Warrant
> > To Sr         Pasthorne for prservacon
> > of ye Game.

## CROMWELL IN WESTMINSTER ABBEY.

The liberal-minded Dean Stanley made what atonement he could for what he rightly described as "the savage ceremonial" of the removal of the bones of Cromwell, and others, from the Abbey, by placing a large tablet in the centre of the apse, engraved as follows :—

In this vault was interred

| | |
|---|---|
| OLIVER CROMWELL | 1658 |
| and in, or near it, | |
| Henry Ireton, his son-in-law | 1651 |
| Elizabeth Cromwell, his mother, | 1654 |
| Jane Desborough, his sister, | 1656 |
| Anne Fleetwood. | |
| Also Officers of his Army and Council. | |
| Richard Deane | 1653 |
| Humphrey Macworth | 1654 |
| Sir William Constable | 1655 |
| ROBERT BLAKE—Admiral | 1657 |
| Dennis Bond | 1658 |
| John Bradshaw, President of the High Court of Justice, | 1659 |
| and Mary Bradshaw, his wife. | |

These were removed in 1661.

By some oversight the body of Lady Claypole, Oliver's favourite daughter, was left in its place, and still remains in the Abbey.

There are few more vexed historical questions than that relating to the ultimate disposal of Oliver's body. One account states that he was buried, at the dead of night, in the Thames; a second, that he lies peacefully buried on the field of Naseby. But the most probable story is, that his son-in-law, Lord Fauconberg and his wife Mary Cromwell, obtained possession of the body after the shameful exposure at Tyburn, and caused it to be buried in their house in Yorkshire, where it still remains. What makes that account the more probable is the known fact that the bodies of Ireton and Bradshaw were removed, as their coffins have been discovered in the vaults of Mugginton Church in Derbyshire.

## CROMWELL'S HEAD.

What is believed, on very good evidence, to be Oliver's head is now in the possession of Mr. Horace Wilkinson, near Sevenoaks, in Kent. A full description of the relic was given (with an engraving) in the *Daily Chronicle* of 6th November, 1895. In a letter to the same Journal, Mr. Frederic Harrison recommended that a committee should be appointed to inquire into the genuineness (or otherwise) of this relic.

## 14 FFEBRUARY ANNO DNI 1645. (†)

These presents doe declare that Richard Downs, Citizen of London, doth undertake a Contract for and agree to and with yᵉ honorable Comᵗᵉᵉ of Lords & Comons for Sʳ Thomas Fairfax, his Army to provide and deliver unto yᵉ said Comᵗᵉᵉ or to such as they shall nominate & appoint the number of yᵉ provisions and at yᵉ rates hereafter specified as followeth.

(vizᵗ·)

Two Thousand Coates & Two Thousand Breeches at seventeene shillings a Coate & Breeches.

Two Thousand paire of stockins at Thirteene pence halfe penny a paire.

The coates to be of a Red Colour, and of Suffolke, Coventry or Gloucester-shire Cloth and to be made Three quarters & a nayle long, faced with bayes or Cotten with tapestrings according to a patterne delivered into yᵉ said Comittee.

The Breeches to be of gray or some other good Colours & made of Reading Cloth or other Cloth in length Three quarters one eighth well lined and Trimmed suitable to y^e patternes presented, the said Cloth both of y^e said Coates and of y^e Breeches to be first shrunke in Cold water.

The stockins to be made of good Welsh Cotten. That although it is impossible for any pson to undertake to make y^e sayd provisions exactly sutable for goodnesse to any patterne for y^t many wil be better and some may be a little worse yet it is y^e resolucon of y^e said Contracto^r and he does hereby promise that as neere as he can none of y^e said provisions of Coates, Breeches & stockins shall be worse then y^e patternes presented to y^e said honorable Com^tee, and that y^e said Com^tee or such as they shall appoint to view & supervise y^e said provisions shall have power to refuse any of them against which there is iust exceptions.

To deliver into y^e said Comittee or such as they shall nominate and appoint one thowsand of y^e said Coates and one thowsand of y^e said breeches and one thowsand of y^e said stockins at or before y^e 21^th day of ffebruary instant and y^e other Moyety of all y^e said pvisions at or before y^e X^th day of March next ensueing.

In Consideracon whereof ye said Com^tee doe Contract and agree to and with y^e said Richard Downs to pay for all the pvisions to the said Richard Downs or to such as he shall appoint one thousand eight hundred and twelve pounds tenne shillings of lawful English money (vixt) for one fourth of y^e said pvisions 453 : ^lb 2s : 6d of like money at the delivery of the said first moyety of y^e said pvisions. And for one fourth thereof being 453 ^b : 2s : 6d of like money at the end of one month after the delivery of the said first moyety of y^e said pvisions. And for one fourth of y^e said pvisions being 453^lb : 2^s 6^d to pay at y^e delivery of y^e second moyety of y^e said pvisions. And for y^e other fourth thereof being 453^lb : 2^s : 6^d to pay at the end of one month after y^e second Moyety of y^e said pvisions.

Att the Com^tee for the
Army the XIIII^th of ffebr. 1645.

This Com^tee doth approve of these Contracts and doe desire that the office^rs of the Ordinance will take notice thereof And carefully see that the Provisions bee answerable to the Agreem^ts. And for as many of the Provisions as they shall receive in and allow to certifie the same unto this Com^ttee.

Rob^t. Boscawen.

## PETITIONS TO OLIVER. (†)

When Oliver "recommended" any course to his Council, or to any other authority, it was only his euphemistic way of saying what the Kings of England said in a more imperative fashion—"Let it be done."

On one occasion a petition was presented to him on behalf of a lad whose mother desired to get him into the Charter-house School, and Oliver endorsed it :

"We refer this petition and certificate to the Commissioners for Sutton's Hospital (Charterhouse), 28th July, 1655."

In reference to this petition Oliver addressed a letter to his Secretary, setting forth the past service the boy's father had rendered to the State, and proceeded : "I have wrote under it a common reference to the Commissioners, but I meane a great deal more, THAT IT SHALL BE DONE, without their debate or consideration of the matter, and so do you privately hint to Mr. ———. I have not the particular shining bauble or feather in my cap for crowds to gaze at, or kneel to, but I have power and resolution for foes to tremble at. To be short, I know how to deny petitions ; and whatever I think proper for outward form to refer to any officer or office, I expect that such my compliance with custom shall be also looked upon as an indication of my will and pleasure to have the thing done ; see therefore that the boy is admitted,

"Thy true Friend,
"OLIVER P."

Evidently, with Oliver there was no compulsion, only they *must.*

Oliver was one of the Governors of the Charterhouse up to the date of his installation as Protector, when General Skippen was appointed in his place.

SESSION OF THE HOUSE OF LORDS.

" This day the Lords kept the fast in the house," 27th January, 1657-58.

From the original MS. in the Author's Collection (Journal of the House of Lords).

## MEETING OF THE HOUSE OF LORDS.

### "WEDNESDAY, 27TH JANUARY, 1657.

(Here follow the names of those present.)

" This day the Lords kept the ffast in the house.

" Dr. Reynolds and Mr. Howe prayed and preached and Mr. Caryll concluded the day with prayer.

" Ordered That the thankes of this house be retorned to Dr. Reynolds for his great paines in helping to carry on the wofke of this day of ffasting and humiliation in this house and that he be desired to print his sermon and he his therein to enioy vsuall p$^r$viledge.

" Ordered That the thanks of this house be retorned to Mr. Howe for his great paines in carrying on the worke of this day of ffasting & humiliation in this house and that he be desired to print his sermon he is therein to enioy the vsuall priviledge.

" Ordered That the thankes of this house be retorned to Mr Caryll for his great paines in carrying on the worke of this day of ffasting & humiliation in this house.

" The Lord Com$^r$ ffyennes declared by direcon of this house this p$^r$sent parliam$^t$ to be Continued vntill nine of the Clock to morrow morning."

The accompanying facsimile of the day's proceedings is from the MS. Journal of the House of Lords in the author's possession. It is interesting from the evidence it gives that the Lords were " ticked off " by placing " pr " opposite their names, as they entered the Chamber.

## JOHN MILTON. (†)

Proclamation by Charles II. for calling in two books written by Milton dated 13th August, 1660—"Pro populo Anglicano Defensio" and an answer to "The Pourtraiture of his Sacred Majesty in his Solitude and Sufferings."

" Whereas John Milton, late of Westminster hath published in print two severall books . . . in both w^h are contained sundry Treasonable passages against Us and our Government and most impious endeavours to justifi the horrid and unmatchable Murther of our late dear father . . . and whereas the said John Milton hath fled or so obscure himselfe that no endeavours used for his apprehension can take effect, whereby he might be brought to a legal Tryall, and deservedly receive condigne punishment for his Treasons and Offences. Now, to the end that our good subjects may not be corrupted . . . with such wicked and Traitorous principles " [and after ordering that all such books shall be delivered up, it goes on] "and the Sheriffs are hereby required to cause the same to be publicly burnt by the hands of the common hangman."

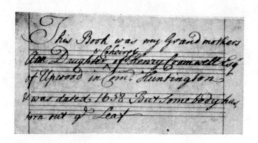

No. 1.

No. 2.

## MANUSCRIPT MUSIC BOOK of ANNE CROMWELL, FIRST COUSIN of OLIVER CROMWELL, (†)

containing a number of pieces. In the original calf binding gilt with clasps and the initials A C stamped on both sides—*folio*.

This intensely interesting volume has a note written on the last page (see illustration No. 1).

The date is 1638, not 1658 as would appear from the reproduction. In the original the figure is seen to be 3.

HENRY CROMWELL was uncle of the Protector, and, doubtless, the book was frequently used by Oliver when he joined his uncle's family circle at Upwood.

On the first leaf in the volume—the only one not ruled in "staves"—is the following quaint design:

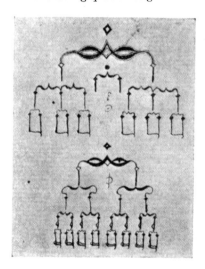

"Fouer moodes in muficke you shall find to bee
But two you only vfe which heare you see
Deuided from the sembreefe is the quauer
Which you with eafe may Larne if yo endauour."

There are precisely fifty pieces in the volume, of which, however, two are duplicates of others. The Staff is ruled in six lines, the musical characters are those of the time, and the book is unquestionably genuine 17th Century.

Many of the pieces are copied in a crude, amateurish fashion, and errors abound. In most such instances the harmonisation is barbarous. On the other hand some are very neatly written and the "arrangement" correct. Doubtless Anne herself copied most of the pieces into the book, while almost certainly others were written by musicians—probably professional men of the time.

The reproduction of the second piece (see illustration No. 2) in the volume—a well-known psalm tune—gives an idea of much of the clumsy harmonisation; while the extract from "The Merry Old Man" affords an instance of the careless, slipshod style of the writing (see illustration No. 3).

On the other hand, the example from "The Healthes" shows neatness and musical character (see illustration No. 4).

Some of the titles are well known: "Besse A Bell," "Daphny," "Fortune my foe," "Frogges Galliard," "In the dayes of old," "The miery Milke-Maide," "The Healthes," etc., etc., though the tunes are not always those given by John Playford and quoted by Chappell. Others are "Mrs. Villar's Sport," "A French Tuckato," "Mr. Ward's Masque," "A Joy," "The Queene's Masque," "The New Nightingall," "An Ayre," "A Corranto," "The Merry Old Man," "The Sheepeard," "The Wiches," "The Scotch Tune," "The Blafing Torch," "Mr Holmes Corranto," "Mr White Lockes Coranto," "Among the Mirtills," "An Almos by Mr. Iue," "A Simphony by Mr Iue," "The Maides," the last piece in the work being "el dono."

Two dismal songs, with words, are "Sweat Sivon songes w^th melody" and "Adeu Adeu O Lett me goe." Mr. Iue is a great favourite and is referred to in the latter song—

> "Sweat Sivon songes w^th melody
> Inchanting Iues w^th Harmon-ey
> Makes all to singe most mery Nots
> O doe not then forfake pooer Oates."

Much light is incidentally thrown on the music, the notation and general character of the writing of the time by the contents of this delightful book, but which there is not space further to refer to here.

(Contributed by my friend G. H. Haswell.)

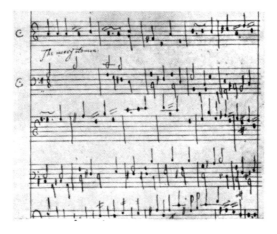

No. 3.

No. 4.

# A MONEY-LENDER'S ADVERTISEMENT,
## *temp :* CHARLES I.

### "AN ABSTRACT OF A DIRECTION CONCERNING REALL CONTRACT.

"Whosoever shall desire to purchase, or put to Sale, to take in Lease, or let to Farme, to Grant, Assigne, Exchange, or otherwise to Contract, or Deale, with or for any Lands, Lease, Rents, Annuities, Mansion-houses, Offices Saleable, or other Estates of what yearly value soever, or to save any such from danger of Forfeiture, through the want of present money : May eyther in their owne names, or in the name of any other trusted by them, have secure meanes with all privacy requisite : for the speedy effecting what shall be desired, in any the Cases aforesayd, or the like : At the Porcht House against St. Andrewe's Church in Holborne, LONDON.

"God save our gracious King Charles."

The ways of Money-lenders seem to be the same in all ages : "absolute privacy," "speedy advances," and no name of lender given. In Charles's time, too, public offices were saleable "properties."

# LETTER FROM CHARLES I.

This is a perfect example of a cryptogram, or secret letter. In Thurloe's collection of State documents there are many examples of this method of communication, but I do not remember if there are any completed ones—*i.e.*, with the elucidations of the cryptic characters filled in by the person to whom the letter is addressed. In this letter of Charles, Lord Asteley has supplied the hidden meaning from his key.

Lo. ASTELEY.

To our right trusty and right welbeloved Jacob Lord Asteley Our Lieutenᵗ Grall of Our Counties of Worcester, Hereford, etc.

CHARLES R.

Right trusty and right welbeloued Wee greet you well. Wee have receaved yoʳˢ of yᵉ 22ᵗʰ, & yᵉ Duplicate of it, And in yᵉ first place Wee give yoᵘ Our thankes for yoʳ extraordinary industry and care in oʳ Services and Affaires committed to yoʳ trust And as Wee approve of all that yoᵘ haue done, soe Wee deoirc yᵉ conliuuance of yoʳ diligence therein Wee haue given Order for a Commission to bee sent yoᵘ to bee Governoʳ of Worcester wᵗʰ power for yoᵘ to make a Deputy, and Wee very well approve of yoʳ choice of

Colonell W as h ing t o n
305 . 459 . 1 . 76 . 129 . 12 . 245 . 52 . 22 . 69 . 4 . 101

to bee yoʳ Deputy, and desire yoᵘ to settle him in it as yoʳ selfe propoundes in yoʳ Lre, and to advise him

to com p ly with our Commissioners
380 146 . 49 . 254 . 409 . 310 . 455 . 33 . 43 . 73 202

for yᵉ good of that Garrison and yᵉ Countrey adjoyning. Wee being resolved not onely to support and countenance

our Commissioner s
305 . 310 . 455 . 36 . 45 . 74 . 4 . 2 . in performance of yᵉ

m b u t
trust Wee haue reposed in the 48 . 2 . 15 . 26 . 54 . 521

to goe t h r o u g h w it
380 . 198 . 52 . 12 . 44 . 24 . 29 . 5 . 13 . 3 . 101 . 76 . 234

h     that   way   of   order   inge
12 . 3 . 387 . 403 . 306 . 315 . 245 Our Affaires in those
partes and in all other places w$^{th}$in Our Quarters, as-
well for y$^e$ ease and good of Our Subjectes as y$^e$
be   for   e   y$^{or}$
advancement of o$^r$ Service 521 . 137 . 174 . 35 . 423
d   e   part   u   r   e   from Worcester.
59 . 34 . 323 . 26 . 44 . 33 . 186 . 621 . 522 . Wee
with   lo:   W   as   h   ing
pray yo$^u$ to take Order 409 . 459 . 76 . 129 . 13 . 245
on   your   D   e   put   y   &   our   Com̃   e
53 . 309 . 4 . 423 . 50 . 34 . 331 . 31 . 1 . 127 . 310 . 455 . 33
r   s   to   in   h   and   the   speed   y
43 . 73 . 3 . 4 . 380 Set 236 . 12 . 127 . 2 . 386 . 371 . 30 . 4
&   per   f   e   c   t   inge   of   the   fortify
repaire 127 . 326 . 61 . 34 . 40 . 53 . 245 . 306 . 386 . 489
c   at   ion   s   t   here   &
40 . 128 . 239 . 73 . 52 . 219 . 202 . 127 especially for
the   f   u   r   n   ish   inge   that   Garison   w$^{th}$
386 . 61 . 26 . 43 . 68 . 243 . 245 . 387 . 497 . 409
good   of   vict$^{lls}$   &   o   t   her
9 . 197 proporcon 306 . 620 . 127 . 22 . 52 . 214
prouisions   a   s   e   i   g   e
569 . 73 against 10 . 1 . 3 . 73 . 34 . 19 . 5 . 36 . 102
If   by   the   fovr   t   h   of
560 . 202 . 237 . 136 . 386 . 192 . 52 . 12 . 2 . 306
the   next   monthe   you   bee   able
386 . 298 . 293 . 422 shall not 137 . 131 . 202 .
to   g   at   her   to   get   her   in   to
380 . 5 . 128 . 214 . 1 . 380 . 199 . 214 . 101 . 236 . 380
b   o   d   y   so   considerable   a strength   of
a 16 . 24 . 59 . 30 . 3 . 356 . 461 . 131 . 1 . 9 . 375 . 306
horse   &   foote   as   you   might   doe
222 . 127 . 181 . 129 . 422 . 290 . 152 . 410 .
by   inge   the   time   for   5   or   6
136 . deferr 245 . 386 . 379 . 174 . 5 . 1 . 307 . 6 . 4
day   s   long   e   r
154 . 73 . 260 . 33 . 43 . 101 . Wee are well pleased,
put   it   off   t   i   l   the
That yo$^u$ 331 . 234 . 306 . 61 . 1 . 52 . 21 . 64 . 3 . 386 .
ten   t   h   of   March :   but   t   h   e   n
110 . 52 . 14 . 306 . 84 . 304 . 135 . 52 . 13 . 34 . 67 .
not   to   f   a   i   l   e   to   mar   c   h
295 . 380 . 61 . 8 . 19 . 64 . 35 . 380 . 279 . 40 . 14 . 1 .
as   as   you   can   to   war   d   vs
129 strong 129 . 422 . 143 . 380 . 625 . 59 . 304 . 306
and   as   man   y   of
127 . Wee desire you to cause 129 . 277 . 30 . 1 . 306 .
yo$^r$   foote   to   bee   m   o   u   n   t   e   d
423 . 181 . 380 . 137 . 46 . 22 . 27 . 69 . 54 . 33 . 60 .

      as      you
4 . 129 . 422 . may possibly. Wee approve of yo^r

      to   p  a  s  the  R  i  u  e  r
advice 380 . 49 . 8 . 73 . 74 . 386 . 43 . 19 . 27 . 36 . 44 .

   at    B  u  r  for  d    &  vp  on
1 . 128 . 1 . 15 . 27 . 44 . 174 . 60 . 3 . 127 . 397 . 309 .

time   ly   not  i   c  e   when  you
379 . 254 . 295 . 18 . 40 . 35 . 2 . 415 . 422 . wilbee

 t  here   wee  shall    the Rendeuous   where
52 . 219 . 1 . 402 . 369 . appoint 386 . 576 . 202 . 413 .

wee  will  haue  our  Force  s  from  the  s  e
402 . 406 . 210 . 310 . 487 . 73 . 186 . 386 . 74 . 34 .

part  s    to  mee    t    &  joy  n  e
323 . 73 . 1 . 380 . 274 . 33 . 52 . 4 . 127 . 240 . 67 . 34

   with  you               The Lord  By  r
2 . 409 . 422 . 202 . 522 . 1 . 2 . 4 . 101 . 386 . 264 . 136 . 43

 o  n   m  u  s   t                  in
24 . 69 . 1 . 46 . 26 . 73 . 53 . 2 . necessarily remayne 236

North Wales  to                 &   to
552 . 622 . 380 . 101  secure those partes . 127 . 380 .

keepe  a    foote inge  t  here  for  vs      if
249 . 10 . 3 . 181 . 245 . 52 . 219 . 174 . 396 . 101 . 237 .

an   y  force  s  shall  from  Ireland
126 . 30 . 487 . 74 . 369 . 186 . 507 arrive

in   our  a  y  d        are  not
236 . 310 . 11 . 30 . 59 . 1 . 410 . whereof Wee 125 . 295 .

out  of   h  o  p  e  though  it  bee
308 . 306 . 12 . 22 . 51 . 34 . 394 . 234 . 137 now late

in  the  yeare          As  for  the  dis
236 . 386 . 425 . 520 . 3 . 2 . 101 . 129 . 174 . 386 . 153 .

order  s  at    b  r  i  d  g  North
315 . 73 . 128 . 202 . 15 . 44 . 19 . 59 . 5 . 552 . 1 Wee

leaue it to yo^u and o^r Com^rs to remedy y^e same in
such sort as yo^u and they shall thinke best for o^r
Service, and Wee shall confirme what yo^u shall
doe therein, as also in y^e rectefying and putting

                    an  y  o  t
into better Order for o^r Service 126 . 30 . 1 . 22 . 52

her Gouernors    with  in  the  pre  c  in  c
214 . 497 . 74 . 409 . 236 . 386 . 327 . 40 . 236 . 42

 t  s    of  your  Comand      such  of
53 . 73 . 4 . 306 . 423 . 456 . 410 . 1 . 305 . 365 . 306

our  Garison  s      as                bee
310 . 497 . 75 . 1 . 129 . yo^u shall thinke fit to 137

kep  t   after  the  pre    force  s  bee  long
249 . 54 . (134 . 386 . 327 sent 487 . 73 . 137 . 260

inge  to  the  m  shall  bee    n  e
245 . 380 . 386 . 47 . 369 . 137 . draw . 67 . 33 . 4 . 1 .

out  to  mar  c  h    with  you  in  to  the
308 . 380 . 279 . 42 . 12 . 1 . 409 . 422 . 236 . 380 . 386

feild             to     put    in     to
193 . 410) Wee would haue you 380 . 331 . 236 . 380 .

the    h   and     s          &     c    harge    of     some
386 . 12 . 127 . 74 . 1 . 127 . 40 . 226 . 306 . 357 .

              s         o    f     the     c     o      u
faithfull person 73 . 1 . 4 . 22 . 61 . 386 . 40 . 22 . 27

n     t     r     e     y        to     bee    he    l     d    for
67 . 54 . 43 . 34 . 32 . 4 . 380 . 137 . 211 . 64 . 60 . 174 .

vs    so    as    they    will             to    man
396 . 356 . 129 . 389 . 406 . vndertake 380 . 277 .

&    keepe         for    vs      with    the     same
127 . 249 . them . 174 . 396 . 2 . 409 . 386 . 367 Contri-

                            to      the   m         here
bucons respectively assignd 380 . 386 46 . 2 . 219

to    for    e     &            C     o    u     n     t
380 . 174 . 34 . 127 secure ye 40 . 22 . 26 . 67 . 52 .

r     y       &   recruit   men    t    here    for
44 . 30 . 1 . 127 . 582 . 276 . 52 . 219 . 174 . or Service

as there Shalbee occasion. Of all yor proceedings

&    m    o     t     ion     s     &     when    wee    may
127 . 46 . 24 . 52 . 239 . 73 . 127 . 415 . 402 . 288

       you    at        B    u     r    for     d      &   with
expect 422 . 128 . 1 . 15 . 26 . 43 . 174 . 59 . 3 . 127 409

what strength
412. 375. Wee desire you to send vs frequent advertisementes.
And soe Wee bid you heartily farewell Given at or Court at
Oxon ye 27th of February 1645

By his Mats Comand

EDW. NICHOLAS.

# INDEX.